Social Work and the Visual Imagination

Images are inscribed in the memory more easily than words, and some remain with the viewer for a lifetime. Combining hindsight, insight and foresight, the chapters in this book turn a spotlight onto various aspects of health, social work and socially engaged arts practice. The visual imagination is evoked in this book to help practitioners see beneath the surface of contentious and problematic issues facing human services today. Risk assessment, child sexual abuse, work-life balance, old age, dementia, substance misuse, recovery, sex work, homelessness, isolation, biography, death and dying, grief, loss, vulnerability, care, and the function of the museum as a preserver of memory, all come under the sustained gaze and examination of the contributors. Grounded in the arts and humanities, the visual sense as a gateway to empathy is explored throughout these chapters. References are included to visual art, curating dramatic performance, poetry, film, dance, photography, diary entries, and public exhibitions. In an age when people increasingly compose their lives by staring into various screens, this book celebrates the visual modality that can humanise services with 'human-seeings'.

This book was originally published as a special issue of the *Journal of Social Work Practice*.

Lynn Froggett is Professor of Psychosocial Welfare at the University of Central Lancashire where she is Co-Director of the Institute for Citizenship, Society and Change. Her professional background is in social work and her research interests include the socially engaged arts in health, welfare, communities and other settings. She is Chair of the Association for Psychosocial Studies.

Julian Manley FRSA researches at the University of Central Lancashire. He is Vice-Chair of the Gordon Lawrence Foundation and on the Executive Committee of the Climate Psychology Alliance.

Martin Smith is an Out of Hours Approved Mental Health Professional. He has researched social workers' experiences of and responses to stress and fear. He is particularly interested in ways in which the Arts can challenge, inform and console in the aftermath of traumatic events experienced by social workers.

Alastair Roy is Professor of Social Research at the University of Central Lancashire and also a member of the Lancashire Institute for Citizenship Society and Change. He has a professional background in Youth and Community Work. His recent work has focused on the development of mobile and visual methods, developed through research which addresses social practice in the arts and community sectors.

Social Work and the Visual Imagination

Seeing with the Mind's Eye

Edited by
**Lynn Froggett, Julian Manley,
Martin Smith and Alastair Roy**

Routledge
Taylor & Francis Group

LONDON AND NEW YORK

First published 2019
by Routledge
2 Park Square, Milton Park, Abingdon, Oxon, OX14 4RN, UK

and by Routledge
52 Vanderbilt Avenue, New York, NY 10017, USA

First issued in paperback 2020

Routledge is an imprint of the Taylor & Francis Group, an informa business

British Library Cataloguing in Publication Data
A catalogue record for this book is available from the British Library

ISBN 13: 978-0-367-66429-9 (pbk)
ISBN 13: 978-0-367-07556-9 (hbk)

Typeset in Perpetua
by RefineCatch Limited, Bungay, Suffolk

Publisher's Note
The publisher accepts responsibility for any inconsistencies that may have
arisen during the conversion of this book from journal articles to book chapters,
namely the possible inclusion of journal terminology.

Disclaimer
Every effort has been made to contact copyright holders for their permission to
reprint material in this book. The publishers would be grateful to hear from any
copyright holder who is not here acknowledged and will undertake to rectify
any errors or omissions in future editions of this book.

Contents

Citation Information   vii

Notes on Contributors   ix

Introduction   1
Lynn Froggett, Julian Manley, Martin Smith and Alastair Roy

1. Looking into the seeds of time. Visual imagery in *Macbeth* and its relevance to social work practice, supervision and research   5
Martin Smith

2. Visual imagination, reflexivity and the power of poetry: inquiring into work–life balance   21
Louise Grisoni

3. Imagining transitions in old age through the visual matrix method: thinking about what is hard to bear   39
Anne Liveng, Ellen Ramvi, Lynn Froggett, Julian Manley, Wendy Hollway, Ase Lading and Birgitta H. Gripsrud

4. Re-imagining dementia using the visual matrix   57
Carrie Clarke

5. Recovery and movement: allegory and 'journey' as a means of exploring recovery from substance misuse   75
Alastair Roy and Julian Manley

6. Walking with Faye from a direct access hostel to her special place in the city: walking, body and image space. A visual essay   91
Maggie O'Neill and Catrina McHugh

7. The cold truth: art as fulcrum for recovery in participants and for civic change   111
Eloise Malone

8. Creative relations   123
William Titley

9. Deleuze, art and social work   135
Lita Crociani-Windland

CONTENTS

10. Accounting for the museum   149
    Myna Trustram

    Afterword   157
    Lynn Froggett, Julian Manley, Martin Smith and Alastair Roy

    Index   159

Citation Information

The chapters in this book were originally published in the *Journal of Social Work Practice*, volume 31, issue 2 (June 2017). When citing this material, please use the original page numbering for each article, as follows:

Introduction

Introduction
Lynn Froggett, Julian Manley, Martin Smith and Alastair Roy
Journal of Social Work Practice, volume 31, issue 2 (June 2017), pp. 117–118

Chapter 1

Looking into the seeds of time. Visual imagery in Macbeth *and its relevance to social work practice, supervision and research*
Martin Smith
Journal of Social Work Practice, volume 31, issue 2 (June 2017), pp. 121–133

Chapter 2

Visual imagination, reflexivity and the power of poetry: inquiring into work–life balance
Louise Grisoni
Journal of Social Work Practice, volume 31, issue 2 (June 2017), pp. 137–152

Chapter 3

Imagining transitions in old age through the visual matrix method: thinking about what is hard to bear
Anne Liveng, Ellen Ramvi, Lynn Froggett, Julian Manley, Wendy Hollway, Ase Lading and Birgitta H. Gripsrud
Journal of Social Work Practice, volume 31, issue 2 (June 2017), pp. 155–170

Chapter 4

Re-imagining dementia using the visual matrix
Carrie Clarke
Journal of Social Work Practice, volume 31, issue 2 (June 2017), pp. 173–188

Chapter 5

Recovery and movement: allegory and 'journey' as a means of exploring recovery from substance misuse
Alastair Roy and Julian Manley
Journal of Social Work Practice, volume 31, issue 2 (June 2017), pp. 191–204

Chapter 6

Walking with Faye from a direct access hostel to her special place in the city: walking, body and image space. A visual essay

Maggie O'Neill and Catrina McHugh

Journal of Social Work Practice, volume 31, issue 2 (June 2017), pp. 207–223

Chapter 7

The cold truth: art as fulcrum for recovery in participants and for civic change

Eloise Malone

Journal of Social Work Practice, volume 31, issue 2 (June 2017), pp. 227–236

Chapter 8

Creative relations

William Titley

Journal of Social Work Practice, volume 31, issue 2 (June 2017), pp. 239–248

Chapter 9

Deleuze, art and social work

Lita Crociani-Windland

Journal of Social Work Practice, volume 31, issue 2 (June 2017), pp. 251–262

Chapter 10

Accounting for the museum

Myna Trustram

Journal of Social Work Practice, volume 31, issue 2 (June 2017), pp. 265–273

Afterword

Afterword

Lynn Froggett, Julian Manley, Martin Smith and Alastair Roy

Journal of Social Work Practice, volume 31, issue 2 (June 2017), p. 275

For any permission-related enquiries please visit:
http://www.tandfonline.com/page/help/permissions

Notes on Contributors

Carrie Clarke is an occupational therapist with Devon Partnership NHS Trust, Exeter, UK. She is an advocate for the development of a compassionate, creative and cultural model of dementia care.

Lita Crociani-Windland is a Senior Lecturer in Sociology and theme leader for Psycho-Social Studies within the Social Sciences Research Group at the University of the West of England, UK.

Lynn Froggett is Professor of Psychosocial Welfare, Co-Director of the Lancashire Institute of Citizenship, Society and Change, and of the Psychosocial Research Unit; also Visiting Professor at the Universities of Stavanger and Roskilde.

Birgitta H. Gripsrud is a Postdoctoral Fellow in the Department of Health Studies at the University of Stavanger, Norway.

Louise Grisoni is Senior Research Fellow in Organisational Studies at the Department of Business and Management, Oxford Brookes University, UK.

Wendy Hollway is Emeritus Professor of Psychology in the Faculty of Social Sciences at The Open University, UK.

Ase Lading is an external Lecturer in the Department of People and Technology at Roskilde University, Denmark.

Anne Liveng is Associate Professor at the Centre for Health Promotions Research in the Department of People and Technology at Roskilde University, Denmark.

Eloise Malone is the Creative Director of Effervescent, a social design and social arts research laboratory based in Radiant Gallery, Plymouth, UK.

Julian Manley researches in Innovation and Enterprise at the University of Central Lancashire, UK.

Catrina McHugh is Artistic Director and writer of Open Clasp Theatre Company, a multi-award-winning women's theatre company based in the north-east of England.

Maggie O'Neill is Chair of Sociology and Criminology in the Department of Sociology at the University of York, UK.

Ellen Ramvi is Professor in the Faculty of Social Sciences in the Department of Health Studies at the University of Stavanger, Norway.

Alastair Roy is Professor of Social Research and Co-Director of the Psychosocial Research Unit at the University of Central Lancashire, UK.

Martin Smith is a Senior Social Work practitioner in an Out of Hours Mental Health Team in Buckinghamshire, UK.

William Titley is a Researcher at the University of Central Lancashire, UK. He is a Senior Lecturer and MA Course Leader in Fine Art.

Myna Trustram works at Manchester School of Art, Manchester Metropolitan University, UK, where she runs a programme of research training and development for PhD students.

INTRODUCTION

Pictures at an edition. The relation between what we see and what we know is never settled. Each evening we see the sun set. We know that the earth is turning away from it. Yet the knowledge, the explanation, never quite fits the sight. (John Berger, Ways of Seeing.)

When the deaths of children known to statutory services are investigated, it has often been found that many were looking, but nobody *saw* the child. We start from the proposition that 'not-seeing' is not a function of vision but a failure of the empathic imagination that follows from prioritizing 'sight' over 'insight'. It is worth noting here, that even when there is insight, this does not necessarily lead to foresight and social workers and others are considered to be at fault when their acts or omissions are looked back on through the lens of hindsight.

Insight which involves the knowledge that arises in the mind's eye is imbued with the sensory capacities of the seer – distilled into the images that we use to call to mind a person, a situation, a predicament. This knowledge does not easily find expression in the verbal language used in professional discourse, and still less in most of the research that underpins the social work knowledge base. Rather, it is a form of 'aesthetic intelligence' grounded in bodily states and expressed through a quality of attention that allows the object to reveal itself – as far as is possible without superimposing extraneous categories of thought, such as those that inform assessment protocols. This kind of intelligence is routinely called into play in encounters between social workers and other helping professionals, and the people they work with. More often than not it is unaccounted for in the records of what they do. In this collection of articles we return to a theme that was introduced by *The Journal of Social Work Practice* nearly a decade ago. Prue Chamberlayne and Martin Smith co-edited a special issue on Art, Creativity and Imagination which was later published as a book (Chamberlayne & Smith 2009).

In the interim years there have been relatively few articles on art and social work practice. It appears that contemporary social work may be suffering from a form of cultural amnesia with respect to its own traditions, documented for example in England's classic text *Social Work as Art*. England (1986) argued that as a relational profession social work should ground itself in the arts and humanities as much as in the social sciences. Much of his work was an attempt to describe the specifically 'artistic' as opposed to generically 'creative' aspects of practice and the book possibly represented a high point for the recognition of aesthetic intelligence within the profession (though this was not a term England specifically used). Some of his concerns were implicitly addressed in subsequent debates on reflective practice and learning, and on critical reflection, although their proponents still conceived reflection primarily as a rational-cognitive process. The emotional dimension of learning and thinking was partly recognized, but the aesthetic was left out of the account. The implications of England's work, it seems, have since been borne out: without the arts and humanities social work fails to recognize and nourish its own 'art'.

In Suzanne Langer's (1948\1942) philosophy of art and music the function of art is de-mystified as a process of 'finding forms for feeling' and this links well with psychoanalytic theories of art and symbolization in the object relations tradition (see for example Glover 2009; Gosso 2004) where the symbol is understood to provide containing form for feeling which is otherwise inexpressible or unthinkable. Some things, as Wittgenstein argued, cannot be *said*, they can only be *shown*. Social workers are often immersed in emotional environments of chaotic and inchoate feeling which evade the possibilities of verbal language and defy rational explanation. Why then would they not value the symbolic potentials offered by the visual arts, poetry and performance?

These art-forms are all represented in this edition where the focus is on the image and the visual imagination, whether it is stimulated by dramatic enactment, figurative speech and writing, or the direct presentation of images themselves. The collection is also a multi-disciplinary and cross-professional compilation: its object is the terrain of social work but the authors come from a number of different backgrounds, each of which offers something distinctive to the field by virtue of the way it works with the visual imagination.

Some of the articles are concerned with the uses of art in practice or organisations by authors with a social work, social pedagogy or consultancy background (Smith, Roy, Manley, Grisoni, Crociani-Windland). Others are produced by authors with a background in socially engaged arts and curating (Mallone, Titley, Trustram). This is a group who are increasingly working in areas such as social care and health care, sometimes alongside professionals – increasingly substituting unintentionally for them in community settings as professional services are reduced. From university based researchers, there is a strong and inventive contribution to visual methods, including articles that use a recently developed group-based method called the visual matrix, based on associative and imagistic thinking (Liveng et al, Clarke, Roy and Manley). This is a method that has been positioned 'between' the arts and social sciences, drawing on both for its development and theoretical foundations. Similarly there are contributions to visual and mobile methods that also use association and image (Roy and Manley, O'Neill and McHugh).

Those readers familiar with Mussgorsky's 'Pictures at an Exhibition' produced in 1874, will be aware that he constructs several musical depictions of works of art hung in a gallery. As the viewer moves from picture to picture Mussgorsky provides a 'promenade' piece of music to describe this transition before going on to musically describe the next picture. We have adapted this idea for the editorial of this special edition of *The Journal of Social Work Practice*. Therefore, rather than follow the established convention of writing an editorial which considers all submissions together at the beginning of an edition and which then goes on to show the contributions one after another, we have arranged articles for this edition as if hung in a gallery in which the viewer enters, comes to the first, walks to the second and so on. Editorial links between the articles are provided by way of brief 'promenade' pieces whereby the reader moves from one contribution to the next. We hope you enjoy the exhibition mounted by this edition and find within it material to surprise, delight, entertain, satisfy, challenge imagination and inspire thought. We begin with an article that thinks about social work through the depiction of emotion in one of Shakespeare's most famous plays.

Note

Editorial references are listed on page 157.

Martin Smith's article uses Shakespeare's *Macbeth* and its visual imagery as a means to discuss social work practice, supervision and research. The article concludes that *Macbeth* might offer something distinctive to busy, hard pressed social workers by opening out a capacity for empathic connection (also explored by Malone in this issue). Smith argues that there is a value to be gained from developing, honing and making explicit the use of imagery in social work, which can help practitioners to reach 'beneath the surface'. This enables social workers to render 'visible' the affective qualities of social work. He shows how *Macbeth* is rich in visual metaphor through which Shakespeare finds a figurative language for otherwise inexpressible emotion.

Turning to social work processes he discusses the ubiquity of risk assessment and the complex temporalities at play in social work, in which practitioners must often generate understandings quickly in the here and now, whilst also orienting themselves towards future possibilities that can't be known or predicted (Gunaratnam 2015). The paper suggests that, rather than being a distraction, the full use of visual sensibility and language which is rich with imagery might allow a fuller truth about social work to emerge. Shakespeare's use of visual language in drama augments the scene on the stage with a scene in the mind offering a window onto the emotional world of the characters that far exceeds their 'actions'. In the discussion of visual matrix methodology later in this issue Liveng et al show how 'a scenic register of experience' conveys a particular depth and complexity of emotion. In social work practice a visual or scenic sensibility may allow unconscious aspects of experience to come to the surface (Roy 2017). The first paper in our collection offers a rich example of this: working with the 'scenic' imagery embedded in language, as Smith does, is a means by which the unconscious dynamics of practice might become better available for thought and communication in practice, supervision and research (Froggett & Briggs 2012).

Martin Smith

LOOKING INTO THE SEEDS OF TIME. VISUAL IMAGERY IN *MACBETH* AND ITS RELEVANCE TO SOCIAL WORK PRACTICE, SUPERVISION AND RESEARCH

This article draws attention to ways in which a close reading of Shakespeare's Macbeth *and careful consideration of its visual imagery can inform social work practice, supervision and research. Elements of social work practice including risk assessment, 'thinking the unthinkable' and disguised compliance are discussed in the context of quotations from the play. The part played by reassurance and the desire to reassure in the supervisory relationship are illustrated in the context of psychodynamic and cognitive-behavioural theories. Examples are cited from both historical research which influenced the formation of Attachment Theory, and contemporary research. These works highlight the importance of looking and seeing and the subsequent value of reflecting on reactions/responses of the viewer to what has been seen. Sleep disturbances and intrusive dreams (pictures of the night) are discussed. The article concludes that close reading and analysis of* Macbeth *have much of value to offer busy social workers.*

Introduction. "And that which should accompany old age …"

Many years ago, when starting out on my social work training, I encountered the ravages of dementia for the first time. One of my placements when qualifying was on a long-stay ward in a psychiatric hospital where I saw shells of older people moving around, perplexed and confused, through the day and the night. People who were physically present but mentally absent, lost 'in a world of their own', lost, trying to find their way back home, lost, in time and space, lost … I read a lot about 'senile dementia' as it was then called, wise words by erudite writers, knowledgeable doctors, experienced medical practitioners. I also read Shakespeare's *Macbeth* (Bevington, Kahn, & Holland 2007). Towards the end of the play, Macbeth is looking back over what has happened to him. He reviews his high hopes, followed by the ever wider-ranging disaster of getting what he thought he wanted along with his increasingly psychotic murderousness to achieve his ends. He comments that he has lived long enough, his way of life has withered and died;

> And that which should accompany old age, / As honor, love, obedience, troops of friends, / I must not look to have, but in their stead, / Curses ... (V, iii, 26–29).

These words resonated me with more powerfully, deeper and for far longer than any of the wise words I read in social work or medical text books. Although the older people I met on the ward had not lived lives anything like Macbeth's, they had reached old age to encounter not honour, but indignity, not love so much as the duty of the staff caring for them, not obedience, but being manoeuvred to conform with what was expected from them, not troops of friends but rarely a single visitor. The 'curses' of dementia replaced the idealised aspects of the wise, benign and respected old age envisaged by Macbeth. Although I could not and cannot explain entirely why, I thought and still think that these words of Shakespeare's 'opened me up' to empathise with the people I was working with in a way that I would not have experienced without them. This was an early indication to me of the influence that Literature generally and Shakespeare particularly can have on those training, working and researching in the caring professions. In this article, I will concentrate on *Macbeth* to illustrate this potential. I begin with a brief plot summary.

Macbeth and his good friend, Banquo return victorious from battle to encounter three witches (weird sisters) on a 'blasted heath' in Scotland. At the time, Macbeth is already Thane of Glamis and the first witch hails him as such. The second witch hails him as Thane of Cawdor and the third witch tells him he "shalt be king hereafter" (I.iii.50). The witches tell Banquo he will not be king himself but that his children will be kings. Shortly after being told by the witches that he will be Thane of Cawdor, this title is bestowed on him by King Duncan. Macbeth writes of his experiences to his wife, Lady Macbeth and they conspire together to kill Duncan as he sleeps in their castle. Macbeth takes the throne and Duncan's sons flee the country. Macbeth has no children so wonders about succession. He fears the predictions the witches made to Banquo so arranges to have him killed. He attempts also to have Banquo's son, Fleance, killed but Fleance escapes. Macbeth fears for his position so goes to consult the witches about his future. They tell him he should beware Macduff (a Scottish lord), that he cannot be harmed by a man 'born of woman' (i.e. by way of a 'natural birth') and that he will not be vanquished until Birnam wood comes to Dunsinane Hill. Attempting to protect his position, Macbeth orders further murders of Lady Macduff and Macduff's children. The consequences of her actions weigh on Lady Macbeth's mind to the extent that she goes mad and kills herself. Eventually, Macduff catches up with Macbeth and kills him. It transpires that Macduff was born by caesarean section.

I now go on to highlight extracts from the play and consider how these have relevance for social work practice, supervision and research. My hope is that by considering the text in some detail it will be possible to reach an enlarged and enhanced understanding of what we do as social workers by way of words which inform and 'open up' our work in a similar way to which the quotation above did for me, all those years ago.

Social work practice. "There's daggers in men's smiles"

Much social work thinking and practice is pervaded by the ubiquity of risk assessment (Gillingham 2016). Will this parent go on to harm (or kill) their child if the child is not removed? Will this person be a danger to themselves and/or others if not detained compulsorily under the Mental Health Act 1983? Will this older person be safe if left alone at home rather than be admitted into full time care? Social workers are frequently attempting to predict the future on the basis of what they know (or think that they know) and what they believe will happen next. Speaking to the witches at the beginning of the play Banquo says to them;

> If you can look into the seeds of time, / And say which grain will grow and which will not, / Speak then to me ... (I.iii.58–60).

Although I am yet to see these words feature in a social worker's risk assessment, essentially, this is what social workers are trying to do – examine the 'seeds of time' to make an informed and considered judgement about which are likely to grow and which to wither.

The witches tell Macbeth three things; he is Thane of Glamis, he is Thane of Cawdor and he shall be king. The three witches represent the past, present and future aspects that should be considered when undertaking risk assessments. Macbeth knows already he is Thane of Glamis. This is 'past' knowledge he already has. At the point at which he meets the witches the King has ordered that he should be made Thane of Cawdor but Macbeth does not yet know this. This represents knowledge that is presently available but, as yet, unknown. The third prediction is the most tricky one. This could happen – and this then raises the question of what social workers might do or might not do to bring about or avoid certain outcomes. Being told that he will be king sets Macbeth on a course which ruins all he has. He has no chance to enjoy the "Golden opinions from all sorts of people" (I.vii.33) that he has recently attracted as a result of his skill and prowess as a soldier. How does the knowledge that something 'might happen' or 'could happen' influence social workers into contributing to bringing into being the possible outcome predicted? Confronted with the need to complete a risk assessment, like Lady Macbeth, social workers are facing an "ignorant present" attempting to "feel the future in the instant" (I.v.53, 54).

The social control aspects of social work centre around the need for safety as a pervading theme and emphasise evidenced-based safe practice. When things go wrong and people are seriously injured or killed, or even when there is a 'near miss' the judgement and risk assessment skills of social workers are called into question, sometimes by means of a Serious Case Review. Once Macbeth is king he reflects on the precariousness of his position and the temporary nature of what he has, "To be thus is nothing; / But to be safely thus. Our fears in Banquo / Stick deep ..." (III.i.47–49). Like Roman emperors and Egyptian pharaohs of old, Macbeth is not satisfied with what he has in the present in this world. He wants to ensure it continues (in the case of the emperors and pharaohs this extended into wanting to see their influence continuing into the afterlife). For social workers, there is always a difficult decision and nuanced risk assessment yet to be made. However accurate, a risk assessment proves to be in relation to a particular person at a point in time there is always another dilemma to face, another risk to be assessed, another decision to be made. In this respect, I recognise Macbeth's wish "to be safely thus" as a heartfelt but unrealistic hope.

In considering the possible outcomes from acting or not acting social workers need to anticipate the consequences of what might result from their decision(s). This entails thinking about what people are, or might be, capable of. In the depiction of Lady Macbeth, Shakespeare shows us a woman and mother thinking of killing her children to get what she wants,

> Come you spirits / That tend on mortal thoughts, unsex me here, / And fill me from the crown to the toe top-full / of direst cruelty. Make thick my blood, / Stop up th' access and passage to remorse, …/… Come to my woman's breasts, / and take my milk for gall, you murd'ring ministers (I.v.37–45).

On hearing details of how some children are tortured, abused and killed by those supposed to be caring for them a common public reaction is expressed in the form of incredulity, 'How could a woman/ mother do that or allow that to happen to her child?' It seems 'unthinkable', beyond belief. In the character of Lady Macbeth, Shakespeare shows it is part of being human to entertain these thoughts as possibilities. She asks to be freed from the limitations of her 'sex' and instead filled up with cruelty so that there is no room left for anything else. She wants remorse and conscience to be obliterated. Earlier on she had chided her husband for being too full of the "milk of human kindness" (I.v.14) and here she wants her own breast milk, that which should enable growth and life, to be turned to gall (bile). This perversion of what might be called a 'maternal instinct' is an example of what Klein (1998) described as the bad breast supplanting the good breast; the breast that restricts and denies supplanting that which sustains and enhances.

Later in the play Lady Macbeth continues,

> I have given suck, and know / How tender 'tis to love the babe that milks me: / I would, while it was smiling in my face, / Have plucked the nipple from his bone- less gums, / And dashed the brains out, had I so sworn as you / Have done to this (1.vii.54–58).

In the play, it is significant that Macbeth and Lady Macbeth have no children. In this extract, Lady Macbeth is referring to a previous child of hers, either one she no longer has any contact with, or a child that has died (and, if so, this suggests the question of how it died). Unusually for her she refers to a state of tenderness and she draws a pic- ture of maternal reverie as a mother breastfeeds a baby who smiles up at her. She then describes pulling the breast from the baby's mouth, thus denying the baby the milk it needs to thrive. Further, she describes going on to smash out the baby's brains having just fed it. Again, in this vivid picture drawn in these few lines Shakespeare shows us the perversion of the maternal instinct, the love that most mothers have, or are expected to have, for their children. The image of corrupted milk re-appears later in the play when Lady Macbeth drugs the possets (warm milky drinks) of the grooms who attend Dun- can while he sleeps, thus making it possible for Macbeth to kill him (II.ii.7).

Blaming social workers when children die is nothing new. The title of Valentine's classic paper, 'The social worker as bad object' (Valentine 1994) which considers denigration of social workers in and by the media in the aftermath of child deaths, written over twenty years ago, brings to mind Klein's 'bad breast'. In Serious Case Reviews, the emphasis is frequently on failures by professionals (usually social workers) to prevent bad things from happening. There is often less emphasis on the capacity a parent or carer might have to harm or kill the child in their care. Recognition and deeper analysis of these tendencies and the thoughts that provoke them would make a welcome addition to the 'lessons learned'.

On discovering the death of Duncan, Macduff cries, "Confusion (i.e. destruction) now hath made his masterpiece!" (II.iii.60). In order to appreciate more fully, the capacity people might have for harming or killing children in their care Freud's concept of the death instinct is helpful. He writes of:

> a force which defending itself by every possible means against recovery and which is absolutely resolved to hold onto illness and suffering ... It is not a question of an antithesis between an optimistic and a pessimistic theory of life. Only by the concurrent or mutually opposing action of the two primal instincts – Eros and the death instinct – never by one or the other alone, can we explain the rich multiplicity of the phenomena of life (Sandler 1991, pp. 29, 30).

The 'Never Again!' headlines in newspapers which are (ironically) repeated over successive years following tragedies of children being killed by those expected to care for them might be set in a more realistic context by a greater recognition of the characteristics portrayed for us in the character of Lady Macbeth. Sometimes social workers and other professionals do fail children they are charged to protect and lessons should be learned and applied from these failures. Sometimes, however, the more destructive and less palatable aspects of being human are responsible, rather than the failures of social workers, and these generally receive less attention. The theme of infanticide continues throughout the play as Macbeth attempts, but fails, to have Banquo's son, Fleance, killed. He orders the deaths of Macduffs children and, even at the end of the play, kills Young Siward, leaving another father mourning the death of a son.

A recurring theme that makes social work particularly difficult and which has been identified in those that go on to harm themselves and/or others is that of 'disguised compliance'. This has been apparent not only in parents/carers of children who have later been harmed or killed but also in mental health service users.

Those caring for a child might give the impression of understanding concerns about that child and being willing to address these concerns when, in fact, they have no real intention of doing so. However, they know it is in their interests to give an impression of compliance so that the Authorities will (wrongly) believe that they are responding appropriately in the best interests of the child. When faced with parents or carers skilled in the arts of subterfuge and deception social workers have been criticised for being too naive, often because they want to believe the best of people and have faith in their capacity for change. This tendency has been referred to as "the rule of optimism" (London Borough of Brent 1985, p. 216). In relation to the quotation from Freud (above) it shows undue emphasis on the life instinct and insufficient awareness of the strength of the death instinct.

Lady Macbeth shows herself to be fully aware of the need to conceal true intentions in order to gain her desired outcome. She criticises her husband for being too easy to 'read' by others, "Your face, my thane is a book where men / May read strange matters" (I.v.58). His face is like 'an open book' which gives too much away about the contents of his mind. She chides him, "To beguile the time (i.e. deceive those around you) /, Look like the time (conform to present practices). Bear welcome in your eye, / Your hand, your tongue. Look like the innocent flower, / But be the serpent under 't" (1.v. 60–63). Social workers are frequently needing to distinguish (risk assess) the extent to which someone is, in fact, an 'innocent flower' or 'the serpent under 't'. Having listened to his wife Macbeth seems to have got the message as he concludes their conversation saying, "mock the time with fairest show, / False face must hide what the false heart doth know" (I.vii.81–82). As a practising mental health social worker, I have interviewed many people who have made suicide attempts who go on to assure those assessing them that they have no intention whatever of repeating these behaviours. With some people these expressed views might be genuine, with others, there is the possibility that they know what those listening 'want to hear' and, if they provide this, they will be under less scrutiny after the assessment and therefore more likely to be left alone and in a better position to make another attempt. Innocent flower or serpent under it? False face hiding false heart? "There's daggers in men's smiles" (II.iii.133). More looking into the seeds of time …

When he sees the witches for the second time they tell Macbeth that he need not fear until Birnam wood comes to Dunsinane hill (IV.i.93). This is a visible indicator of something moving from where it once was to somewhere different in such a way that can be clearly seen. Social workers are rarely able to observe anything so obvious. Changes and possible changes are frequently nuanced, indistinct, ambiguous and uncertain. It is hard to know what is 'really going on' and for this reason it can be helpful to talk to a trusted colleague when attempting to determine and weigh up risks and ascertain a way forward. A mechanism provided for social workers by which they might be able to do this is supervision and the supervisory relationship is now considered.

Supervision. "A foolish thought to say a sorry sight"

In the earlier parts of the play, there is a sense in which Lady Macbeth operates in a supervisory role in relation to her husband. Macbeth doubts that he is capable of killing Duncan, "If we should fail?" Lady Macbeth responds firmly, "We fail! / But screw your courage to the sticking place (notch on a crossbow that holds the string taut) / And we'll not fail" (I.vii. 58–60). She tells him to have faith and show courage, he might doubt himself but he has the capability for the task, he just needs to believe in himself sufficiently. Supervisors of social workers often want to help their supervisees to grow and develop their skills so that they can extend the repertoire of what they believe themselves to be capable of achieving. Supervisors need to try and find a way of providing genuine and effective encouragement rather than false re-assurance which doesn't convince or endure. Lady Macbeth was only partly effective in her supervision as Macbeth returns from killing Duncan still carrying the daggers he used. He refuses to return them, leaving her to do this. His expressed concern about the possibility of failure seeps into his ability to act as he wants to.

Having killed Duncan, Macbeth regrets what he has done and seen, "This is a sorry sight". Ever the pragmatist at this stage in the play, Lady Macbeth retorts, "A foolish thought, to say a sorry sight" (II.ii.2223). Here Shakespeare could be seen as anticipating the essence of cognitive behavioural therapy – change your thoughts and you'll see things differently. She continues, "Consider it not so deeply" (II.ii.32) as if it's simply a matter of deciding not to think about something in too much detail. I was recently working with an 84 year old woman with dementia who was in a Nursing Home. Aged 10, this woman was one of only two survivors of an air raid shelter, bombed in the Second World War. One hundred and fifty-one people had died in this bombing, including several of the woman's close family. Since being in the nursing home she continued to regularly re-experience this event by way of flashbacks which caused her to repeatedly look again at the horror she had seen. It might be a foolish thought to say a sorry sight but this did not help her.

When researching social workers' experiences of distress (Smith & Nursten 1998) I found that when social workers had experienced traumatic events one of the most profoundly unhelpful responses they recalled was when supervisors and managers under-estimated and 'played-down' the significance and repercussions of the event as they had experienced it. Returning to the office having been threatened or involved in a 'near miss' workers described responses like, "Well nothing happened did it? You're still here and OK aren't you?" While these statements were true they entirely missed the emotional and psychological impact of what might have happened ... One of the strengths of a psychodynamic perspective is that it looks beneath and cautions against groundless re-assurance which serves no good purpose and leaves people feeling misunderstood rather than empowered. I frequently recall the dictum, 'Reassurance never reassures' and attempt to hold onto this when feeling an impulse to reassure a worker I am supervising (Malan 1979; Smith 2000).

Macbeth looks down at his blood-stained hands and laments, "Will all great Neptune's ocean wash this blood / Clean from my hand?" His wife is contemptuous of his 'moaning' and tells him, effectively to not be so stupid and pull himself together, remarking, "My hands are of your colour, but I shame / to wear a heart so white, A little water clears us of this deed. / How easy is it ... Be not lost / So poorly in your thoughts" (II.ii. 60–74). She later chides him further along these lines, "Things without all remedy / Should be without regard. What's done is done" (III.ii.1213).

In their differing responses, Macbeth and Lady Macbeth show the different extremes of positions social workers can adopt when things go wrong or there is concern they might go wrong. Macbeth provides an example of 'catastrophic thinking' – it's all ruined, nothing can help, my hands are stained with blood so deeply that all the water from all the oceans in all the world would not be sufficient to get them clean. Lady Macbeth, by contrast, tells him there is no need to exaggerate or get things out of proportion as a little water is all that's needed to make their blood-stained hands clean again – "all shall be well, and all shall be well, and all manner of thing shall be well" (Julian of Norwich 1966, p. 35). These two responses that might be taken to a supervisor also mirror possible views of risk assessment. One view being that the worse imaginable outcome will ensue so the greatest possible protective measures need to be put in place, the other that things will work out OK, a situation can essentially be left alone with need for no, or only minimal intervention. There is a third view between these two and this is the ideal position to aim for in risk assessment and supervision. This is the view that takes a realistic, informed and measured account of risks inherent in a situation, does justice to them but does not allow them to get out of hand in such a way that exaggerates their influence.

Klein (1988) referred to the first of these positions as the paranoid schziod position where a person fears that everyone (and sometimes everything) is against them, plotting against them, intending them ill, wanting to bring them down, disadvantage them, harm them, maybe even kill them. Macbeth provides a further example of this when he hallucinates Banquo's ghost. He turns on those present at the feast and questions, not, 'Why has this happened?' or 'What's going on here?' but "Which of you have done this?" (III.iv.48). The third position described above is what Klein has named the depressive position and this is the balanced view that acknowledges that there is the potential for good and bad in most people and most situations. Because the degree of good and bad will vary from time to time a realistic and informed view should be taken about what's going on and what might happen. Sensitive supervision can help social workers move closer to the depressive position and thereby achieve an appropriate reading of a difficult situation they have encountered or decision that they face without falling into the equal and opposite traps of either over- or under-estimating these.

Lady Macbeth's comment, "A little water clears us of this deed" is frequently cited as an example of dramatic irony. As the play progresses, she changes from unscrupulous, demonic "fiend-like queen" (V.vii.99) to a destroyed woman, unable to sleep or function who later kills herself as she cannot escape the mental consequences of what she has done. She needs a light next to her continually through the darkness and obsessively washes her hands while sleep walking, claiming, "Here's the smell of the blood still. All the perfumes of Arabia / will not sweeten this little hand" (V.i.3940). Her reference to 'all the perfumes of Arabia' recalls Macbeth's earlier mention of 'all great Neptune's ocean' in its all-encompassing, catastrophic scope. People can move from paranoid schizoid to depressive position and back again and good supervision will help them to recognise this. I have benefitted from a co-supervision arrangement with a trusted colleague over many years. When we reflected recently on pervading and recurring themes, we have brought and continue to bring to our discussions, we noted we are often essentially trying to help the other move from a paranoid schizoid position, nearer to a depressive position.

Another way in which social workers might be helped to see things in different ways is by way of research, both by undertaking this research themselves and by reading the research of others.

Research. "The very painting of your fear"

Having ordered Banquo to be killed Macbeth sees his ghost sitting in a seat at a feast he has arranged when others present see the seat to be unoccupied. He shouts at the ghost. Lady Macbeth (still the strong, dominant force at this stage in the play) rebukes him, "This is the very painting of your fear .../... Impostors to true fear" (III.iv.60–63). She tells him that looking at a painting should not be frightening as it is not 'true' fear but merely a representation of it. This rebuke echoes a comment earlier in the play just after Macbeth has killed Duncan when Lady Macbeth chides him, "'Tis the eye of childhood that / Fears a painted devil" (II.ii.56). Throughout *Macbeth* Shakespeare draws (!) attention to the importance of visual images. Prior to hallucinating Banquo's ghost and before killing Duncan Macbeth had previously hallucinated a dagger and asked himself whether he is actually seeing a real dagger or "A dagger of the mind, a false creation". He continues, "Mine eyes are made the fools o' th' other senses, / Or else worth all the rest" (II.i.39–45). (i.e. Either my eyes have tricked all my other senses, or, only my eyes are telling the truth). How much can people believe what they see, particularly when they might be seeing things in or through their mind's eye?

When researching social workers' experiences of distress (Smith & Nursten 1998) several participants told me that most disturbing for them was not what was actually happening but what they 'saw' in their imagination as it 'ran riot'. One worker interviewed a service user and looked down to a bag the service user carried in which she could see the handle of a ceremonial sword sticking out. In her mind's eye, she 'saw' herself being cut in half by this sword. Another worker visited an address where there were apparently dangerous dogs, out of control. Once away from the home, she later 'saw' these dogs turning on the children in the house, blood dripping from their jaws. Another worker was shut in a room with several children and felt threatened by them. She thinks there were probably seven or eight children there but said, "in my darkest thoughts, I seem to think there were dozens of them". Her mind's eye had showed her a more frightening picture than the reality. Her 'painting' of the fear was worse than the real thing. For another worker, the visual sense brought back to mind a tragic event as a mother he had worked with jumped from a building killing both herself and the baby she held in her arms when she jumped. The worker said every time he saw the building she had jumped from, he recalled this event.

I became particularly interested in what social workers 'saw' and how this informed and influenced their work so when researching social workers' experiences of fear (Smith 2005) one question I asked as part of a semi-structured interview was 'If you were looking at a picture entitled 'Fear in social work' what would you see'? The intention behind asking this question was to appeal to the visual in workers in addition to the rational / verbal / descriptive responses that were provided to other questions. Dalley (1984, p. xiii) stresses that our visual sense is crucial because,

> Man's most fundamental thoughts and feelings, derived from the unconscious, reach expression in images rather than words … every individual, whether trained or untrained in art, has a latent capacity to project his inner conflicts into visual form.

Seeing, as well as hearing and writing, has an important place in social work traditions. When James and Joyce Robertson saw the extent of distress caused for young children as a result of being separated from their mothers on hospital wards in the 1940s they thought the scale of this distress to be so extreme it could not be justified and that hospital practices should be changed. Their way of campaigning for what they believed was novel as, rather than attempt to argue and persuade verbally or put their views in any one of several written forms, James Robertson filmed the distress of some of these children and showed the films to relevant others. He comments on his reasons for using film as a means of influence,

> Our way of focusing attention on the problem was to turn to narrative film … presentation on film gives the nearest approximation to actuality and the visual medium is much more effective than the spoken or printed word in piercing resistance in the field of child care (Robertson 1989, p.4).

Not only was their work and their means of promoting it ultimately effective in leading to changes in hospital; policy but it also had a profound influence on John Bowlby and his subsequent development of Attachment Theory. Bowlby comments on the back of their book,

> James Robertson achieved great things … His sensitive observations and brilliant filming made history, and the courage with which he disseminated – often in the face of ignorant and prejudiced criticism – what were then very unpopular findings, was legendary. He will always be remembered as the man who revolutionized children's hospitals … I am personally deeply grateful for all that he did.

These films had more influence than a thousand academic papers and went on to launch a thousand changes.

More recent examples of the use of the visual in social work include Hartley and Lee's account (2013) of running workshops for public sector staff faced with a time of uncertainty and change. The authors were managers of community mental health teams and wanted to help a frightened and demoralised work force express their feelings about proposed cuts and changes within their service. Instead of delivering a 'Powerpoint' presentation with bullet points the authors opted instead to show those attending the workshop pictures by Bosch, Rousseau, Breughel and Goya. They then went on to facilitate discussions about the feelings these works gave rise to and the relevance of these thoughts and feelings to the situation the workers faced. When researching the views of mental health social workers in Northern Ireland concerning religion and spirituality, as part of her research method, Carlisle (2016) invited participants to bring an object to the research interview which expressed, if anything, what religion and spirituality meant to them. Again, there is the emphasis on starting with what can be seen and going on to discuss the feelings this evokes in the viewer.

Several social workers I spoke to throughout my research reported that experiences of fear and distress intruded on their ability to get to sleep. Others fell asleep and were later disturbed by images which featured in troubling dreams. One worker repeatedly woke at night to 'see' the face of a woman she had worked with who had been killed by her husband. *Macbeth* has much to say about the importance of sleep and the difficulties raised when sleep is interrupted.

Returning from killing Duncan Macbeth tells his wife,

> Methought I heard a voice cry, "Sleep no more! / Macbeth does murder sleep". The innocent sleep, / Sleep that knits up the raveled (i.e. unraveled) sleeve of care, / The death of each day's life, sore labour's bath, / Balm of hurt minds, great nature's second (main) course, / Chief nourisher in life's feast. (II.ii.37–42)

I have spoken to many social work colleagues over the years who have lost sleep, worrying about possible consequences arising from decisions they have made or not made. They know the feeling of seeing the work they have attempted fall to pieces like a 'sleeve of care' that unravels before their wide-awake eyes in the early hours and which will not be knitted back together again. There is no soothing bath for their sore labour, no calm for their hurt minds and the anxieties of the next day are made worse by lack of nourishing sleep, which leads to fuzzy thinking, sluggish responses and poorer decision-making.

Macbeth cannot rest, "Full of scorpions is my mind, / ... the affliction of these terrible dreams shake us nightly" (III.ii.1937). Later in the play, commenting on Lady Macbeth's sleep-walking the Doctor observes, "Unnatural deeds / Do breed unnatural troubles. Infected minds / to their deaf pillows will discharge their secrets" (V.i.57–59). Things seem worse at night and the image of the unhearing and unresponsive pillow as therapist / counsellor / confessor will ring true for many social workers who struggle with "thick-coming fancies / That keep them from rest" (V.iii.39).

Conclusion. "Canst thou not minister to a mind diseased?"

It is part of Shakespeare's remarkable achievement in *Macbeth* that for all of his savagery, blood-lust, murderous and psychotic behaviours Macbeth somehow remains a character who continues to inspire interest and even sympathy in those reading and watching the play. Of all the poignant speeches Shakespeare has given to his various characters he gives one of the most tender of all to Macbeth as he laments his wife's mental illness just before her suicide when he says to the Doctor,

> Cure her of that. / Canst thou not minister to a mind diseased, / Pluck from the memory a rooted sorrow, / Raze out the written troubles of the brain, / And with some sweet oblivious antidote / Cleanse the stuffed bosom of that perilous stuff / Which weighs upon the heart? (V.iii.40–45)

I find myself recalling this speech often when talking to relatives of people suffering extremes of mental illness, particularly those who have been struggling with these issues over many years. It stays in my mind not only because of the meaning of the words used and the content of the speech but also because of its rhythm, tone and pace. Many different sorts of medication and various interventions have been tried and failed yet still the person is no better. There is something in these words that portrays the weariness of a struggle over a long time; The feeling that nothing can help but also the still remaining, flickering desire / hope that there might yet be something that could help. The wish that it could be so simple as to 'pluck from the memory a rooted sorrow' as if it were a weed that could simply be pulled up and thrown away. The longing that 'written troubles of the brain' could be merely wiped away in a single motion and that there somewhere exists a 'sweet oblivious antidote' that could take effect and bring about an immediate transformation when all other potions and medicines have been tried and failed.

Near the end of the play when Macbeth hears that his hopes for a remedy for his wife have been dashed and she has died, apparently by killing herself, he responds with one of the best known speeches from the play,

> Tomorrow, and tomorrow, and tomorrow, / Creeps in this petty pace from day to day / To the last syllable of recorded time, / And all our yesterdays have lighted fools / The way to dusty death. Out, out, brief candle, / Life's but a walking shadow, a poor player / That struts and frets his hour upon the stage / And then is heard no more. It is a tale / Told by an idiot, full of sound and fury, / Signifying nothing (V.v.19–28).

As an economic and yet remarkably poignant expression of regret, despair and futility this is unsurpassed.

Faced with the prospect (and/or reality) of too few people to complete too many tasks, responding to investigations, inspections, Serious Case Reviews and complaints, attempting to meet performance targets and imminent statutory deadlines, some will question where they might find the time to read, watch and reflect on *Macbeth*. I have found making the time to do this more than worthwhile. The play resonates with a relevance that remains for me as a social work practitioner, supervisor, and researcher, from the 'seeds of time' at the beginning, to the 'last syllable of recorded time' at the end.

References

Bevington, D., Kahn, M., & Holland, P. (Eds.). (2007). *Macbeth. Shakespeare in performance*. London: Methuen.

Carlisle, P. (2016). Religion and spirituality as troublesome knowledge. The views and experiences of mental health social workers in Northern Ireland. *British Journal of Social Work, 46*, 583–598.

Dalley, T. (Ed.). (1984). *Art as therapy. An introduction to the use of art as a therapeutic technique*. London: Tavistock.

Gillingham, P. (2016). Predictive risk modelling to prevent child maltreatment and other adverse outcomes for service users. Inside the 'Black Box' of machine learning. *British Journal of Social Work, 46*, 1044–1058.

Hartley, C., & Lee, C. (2013). Can art-based reflection help us cope with organisational change in the public sector? *Journal of Social Work Practice, 27*, 441–453.

Julian of Norwich. (1966). *Revelations of divine love*. London: Penguin.

Klein, M. (1988). *Envy and gratitude and other works 1946–1963*. London: Virago.

Klein, M. (1998). *Love, guilt and reparation and other works 1921–1945*. London: Vintage.

London Borough of Brent (1985). *A child in trust. The report of the panel of inquiry into the circumstances surrounding the death of Jasmine Beckford*. Middlesex: Author.

Malan, D. (1979). *Individual psychotherapy and the science of psychodynamics*. London: Butterworth- Heinemann.

Robertson, J. (1989). *Separation and the very young*. London: Free Association Books.

Sandler, J. (Ed.). (1991). *On Freud's "Analysis terminable and interminable"*. New Haven, CT: Yale University Press.

Smith, M. (2000). Supervision of fear in social work. A re-evaluation of reassurance. *Journal of Social Work Practice, 14*, 17–26.

Smith, M. (2005). *Surviving fears in health and social care. The terrors of night and the hours of day*. London: Jessica Kingsley.

Smith, M., & Nursten, J. (1998). Social workers' experience of distress – Moving towards change? *British Journal of Social Work, 28*, 351–368.

Valentine, M. (1994). The social worker as bad object. *British Journal of Social Work, 24*, 71–86.

Although written as a play intended primarily for performance 'Macbeth' includes a great deal of poetry which connects with resounding force. The 'poetic truth' of the words, phrases, expressions and speeches linger long in the mind. In the article that follows Louise Grisoni expands on the transformative effects that poetry can offer. She acknowledges that poetry's reputation can be one of inaccessibility, exclusivity, and rarification, removed from everyday life experience. However, she goes on to show that because of its compact and compressed form a telling metaphor or combination of words can say or show as much as, if not more than, a far wordier novel. Grisoni uses poetry as a form of inquiry and runs poetry-inspired workshops, perhaps as a part of an organisation's staff development programme. She not only inspires the creation of poems that represent and speak to people's experiences but also enquires into the meaning of the poems created. She provides a loose structure and within this encourages the use of free association, popularised by Freud and later psychoanalysts. In this article Grisoni concentrates particularly on a poetic exploration of the stated importance of a work-life balance within a change management context. Poetry workshops were offered on a voluntary basis to those who wanted them. She provides an example of a 'collective poem' from which images and metaphors emerge, speaking to experience. A shape and visual sense is given to strong, perhaps partially recognised, feelings. The structure rhythm, pace and tone of the poem all contribute to its impact and resonance. The article concludes that while the Government is seen to encourage employers to promote the importance of a work-life balance the lived experience is that this is often unattainable, leaving feelings of dissatisfaction and failure in its wake as it disappears, out of view and out of reach. Busy, stressed and stretched social workers and their managers will find much to relate to in this article. They may even be inspired to write something, perhaps collectively.

The notion that poetry is there to be turned to in our darkest hours of greatest need is illustrated by books such as 'The Emergency Poet: An Anti-Stress Poetry Anthology' edited by Deborah Alma (2015, Michael O'Mara Books, London), and '101 Poems to get you through the day and night: A Survival Kit for Modern Life' edited by Daisy Goodwin (2000 Harper Collins, London). An appreciation of poetry that speaks to or for us can help us to see something a little more clearly and, if we can see, anything at all, the darkness must be receding, if only a little.

Louise Grisoni

VISUAL IMAGINATION, REFLEXIVITY AND THE POWER OF POETRY: INQUIRING INTO WORK–LIFE BALANCE

This article explores the use of visual imagination and reflexivity in the creation of poetry as a form of action inquiry. The power of poetry to help inquire into and illuminate new understandings is demonstrated in the creative and imaginative use of imagery, similes and metaphors contained within the choice of words and the connections made to them. Through my work with managers and staff in organisations, using poetry I have come to understand that the poetic words used not only hold the possibility of explaining and describing experiences, they validate the range of associated emotions and can also influence actions when new meanings and understandings are reached. I have found that the process of action inquiry encourages and facilitates reflexivity. For the purpose of this article I have chosen to focus on work-life balance – an issue that many find challenging at different stages in their working lives.

Introduction

Poetry is often thought to be something that is inaccessible and not particularly part of everyday life experience. However, interest in arts-based approaches, including the use of poetry in organisational research has been growing (Darmer & Grisoni 2011; Morgan, Lange, & Buswick 2010; Grisoni 2008, 2009). In this article I suggest that exploring organisational and personal challenges associated with work–life balance through the medium of poetic inquiry, can generate new insights, understandings and actions. The imagery generated in poetic inquiry is wide ranging and can offer exploration of difficult or frustrating challenges. Poetic language is full of metaphor and simile and it is through reflexive engagement with the words used that we are able to generate new actions and understandings. As I argue elsewhere poetry: 'is a powerful medium, as it can capture the richness of language and harness reflective processes that encourage expression of the complexity of organizational experience' (Grisoni 2008, p. 111). Using poetry can bring to life and problematise an issue giving rise to fresh ways of thinking which includes an understanding and recognition that meaning is provisional, changes over time, and is ambiguous and uncertain. In working with poetry we are encouraged to make associative connections, question givens and seek less obvious connections which help make sense of our experiences.

In earlier work (Grisoni & Kirk 2006) I have found that poetry helps bring together unconscious and deliberative ways of knowing, providing an opportunity to influence organisational behaviour and management practice. I identify that the power of the poem lies in its ability to focus in not only on factual details but also on behavioural and affective elements and cite Whyte (1994) who talks of 'the fierce unremitting wish for the dangerous truth that is poetry's special gift' (1994, p. xv). I argue that poems can reveal hidden aspects of organisational life:

> The ability of poetry to get to the essence of an event or episode opens up an opportunity for greater understanding as well as the potential for change in individuals and organisations (Grisoni & Kirk 2006, p. 513).

This opportunity for greater understanding and change is a feature of reflexive practice which has been identified as an important factor in support of ethical and competent professional practice. The understanding of reflexivity that is used in this article is that it moves beyond reflection to include the influence of underlying values, assumptions and beliefs and to critically consider their impact on perceptions of experience and subsequent actions. Using action inquiry to help unscramble meaning in the poems ensures that the processes of reflexivity are activated with the potential to influence professional practice.

This paper will focus upon the creation of collaboratively generated poems, using action inquiry as an enabler of reflexive practice, exploring how this process promotes personal and professional development. I will demonstrate how writing poetry stimulates visual inquiry by working with metaphor and imagery leading to new understandings and insight. The personal and organisational dilemma that will be examined in some detail relates to experiences of Work-life-Balance – an issue that many struggle with and feel challenged by.

Why action inquiry?

According to Torbert (2004) action inquiry as a lifelong process of transformational learning that individuals, teams and whole organisations can undertake if they wish to become increasingly capable of listening into the present moment from which the future emerges, increasingly alert to the dangers and opportunities of the present moment; and increasingly capable of performing in effective, transformational and sustainable ways. Action inquiry works at different levels as a research process: at an individual level the emphasis is on effectiveness and integrity, at an interpersonal level critical and constructive mutuality is an important aim and at organisational and societal level sustainability is the goal. Taken together these three levels create the opportunity for transformation which requires a willingness to be vulnerable and to transform oneself. At the heart of action inquiry is a recurring action-reflection cycle predicated on the relationship of improved knowledge through action, and new or revised action based on imaginative reflective learning (Ellis and Kiely 2010). The process of inquiry is responsive to the needs of participants and can change shape and direction as understanding about what is really happening and what is really important changes and grows. The emergent inquiry process is undertaken in the spirit of collaboration and co-inquiry.

Action inquiry also facilitates the questioning of how our own assumptions are constructed and allows us to learn about and challenge our thinking. This questioning of assumptions embodied in theory and practice is integral to all action inquiry strategies. According to Ellis and Kiely (2010 p. 89) the overall purpose of action research is to create the appropriate conditions to solve work-based situations and problems within the context of a cyclical inquiry process. In addition action research also aims to making change and learning a self-generating and self-maintaining process. In participatory action research a collaborative relationship between the researcher and subjects is a central focus Participatory action research seeks to bring about change in the lives of people that they themselves initiate.

Working with poetic action inquiry

Over the years I have run a range of poetry inspired workshops: sometimes where participants are invited to attend as part of staff development activities within a single organisation; some are stand alone activities open to a specific audience (e.g. women's networks); and some are where I work with academic co-researchers to join me in exploring the creation of poetry and inquiry into meaning (e.g. ESRC Festival of Social Science 2016, academic conferences such as the Art of Management and Organisation conferences). When I started working with poetry as a form of inquiry, over 15 years ago I found very few people had positive memories of or connections to poetry. Many spoke of having to memorise poems at school and that had turned them off. Others said they couldn't connect to poetry as the meanings were too hidden for them. I now find that many of those drawn to attend the workshops and events I organise have written their own poetry and are much more open to experiment with this form of inquiry. To explore the issues and access the lived experience of participants in the workshop I select from the wide range of poetic forms such as free writing, haiku, black out poetry, blank verse, sonnets etc. depending on the experience of the group and my sense of the general enthusiasm for poetry among participants.

As I have refined and developed my practice, the process I have developed for the creation of poems takes the form of action inquiry with emphasis not only on creating poems but also on inquiring into the meaning of the poems. The focus of the inquiry is agreed with participants attending the workshops who are invited to discuss their experiences and what the topic means to them. At this point I have found that it is useful to include some embodiment exercises to experience the impact of the concept in a holistic way. This helps workshop participants move from intellectualising the topic to the personal experience of what it feels like and builds trust and openness in the group. Asking questions such as: Can you make a shape to represent work–life balance? What does work–life balance feel like to you? Where do you feel tension, heaviness in your body? What happens when you move? This process helps open participants to a different range of experiential knowing which helps activate creative imagination. Next, I introduce the idea that there is a need to find new ways to address flexible responses, innovation and knowledge creation in times of unpredictability and instability which has provoked calls to take inspiration from the arts (Knowles & Cole 2008). We talk a little about poetry and experiences of writing and reading poetry. Depending on how long the event is participants are asked to bring along and read a favourite poem or something they have written themselves to share. These introductory activities help set the context and mood for the workshop: asking that participants will work with their experiences and emotions, access their imagination and will appreciate how others see and feel differently.

For those with very little experience haiku provides a useful form as there are clear guides for the number of syllables and lines that structure the poem (Grisoni 2009). The 'corps exquis' form is another poetic form particularly suited to collaborative writing and shared exploration of an organisational issue or problem (see Grisoni 2008, p. 118). The aim is to facilitate multiple voices, readings and understandings of what is produced and be surprised by unanticipated connections (Grisoni 2009; Page, Grisoni, & Turner 2014). Working with groups of up to 8 participants, I tend to provide a loose structure for each line such as: first line – consider what the issue is like (encouraging imagery, simile or metaphor); next line – free associate to the key word given; next line – how does it feel (encouraging emotion); next line – ask a question; next lines – free associate (promotes more imagery), last line – offer an alternative or action (promotes reflexivity). After each person has written their line they fold the paper over and write a key word as a prompt for the next person to generate their line of poetry. This writing of one line, folding and choosing a key word continues until everyone has written 8 lines (depending on the number in the group). At this point the paper has found its way back to each person who wrote the first line and the poem can be revealed (it sounds complicated but isn't in practice!). Here is an example of abstracts from collective poems created at the 2007 poetry and poetics stream of the Art of Management Conference with the focus on working with poetry as arts-based method of research:

Collective poem: where each line is written by a different person	Key word prompts
In the room the people come and go	Room
Room for laughter	Laughter
It's fun and games alright	Alright
Together we create, re-create	Re-create
something new and something old	
Make again, engender, conceive, co-create	Co-create
Co-create, re-create, calculate	Calculate
Being here, hot, hopeful	Here
Here and now, now and here, nowhere	Now
Now and again I feel here and now	Feel
Summertime becomes a silent surprise	Silent
Still, quiet, withdrawn	Withdrawn
Inside my heart – more precious thoughts	Heart
There's no bypass for this	This
Out of the box, out of the role, beyond the rules	Role

The joy of this method is that not only are collective poems created reflecting a collective perspective, but participants can reconstruct their own lines and discover the poem they did not know they had written. Here is my poem extracted from the collective poems (two lines of which are contained in the examples above):

Being here, hot, hopeful

Desire to be alive, make a difference
Connections and memories, forgotten and remembered
Confusing opposites and more
Together we create, re-create something new and something old
Who has the answers we seek?

Presented without further explanation the poems appear intriguing but perhaps of limited value and use. It is only on further reflexive inquiry into what meanings the poems hold for individuals and groups that a fuller appreciation is developed. The richness of images and associations contained in the poems when combined with reflexive sense-making encourages new insights and offers the potential for individual and organisational change.

One area of concern that sometimes emerges from participants in engaging with arts-based approaches such as poetry relates to concerns about the quality (and by implication relevance) of the work produced. Lafreniere and Cox (2012) in their work to develop a framework for the assessment of arts-based works suggest that 'An example of a relevant quality of a research poem … would be the vividness with which the poem conjures an image, sound or feeling' (2012, p. 321). Throughout this paper the poems have provided vivid imagery directly based as they are in the experiences of participants and in addition they have provided plenty of opportunity to generate new questions and inspiration for dialogue (Siegesmund & Cahnmann-Taylor 2008). In terms of incorporating reflexivity into the inquiry process it therefore becomes important for participants to work with each other where the assumptions of deficiency and negativity have taken hold presenting work–life balance as an impossible task for those facing a range of life challenges and choices. To access this level of insight and self-discovery requires a level of trust. This is established during the workshop where time is given to review the poems. Participants develop skills of inquiry into the poems assisting others and themselves in their processes of reflection and developing reflexivity moving the activity of generating poems beyond word play into serious consideration of applications of new insights into life contexts. Working reflexively with action inquiry requires questioning and capturing 'the complex, interactional and emergent nature of our social experience' (Cunliffe 2003, p. 984). In this way we can work with differing interpretations of and meanings ascribed to understandings of work–life balance which is the focus of this paper.

The challenges of work–life balance

The question of work–life balance is topical and closely associated with the area of 'well-being' in the workplace as organisational life increasingly features high levels of stress and illness. It can be broadly defined as a set of work-based policies and practice to help individuals to achieve a balance between the demands arising from paid work and their personal lives. When it was introduced by Government in the UK during the 1970's the term related principally to employers and the work context with the introduction of flexible working practices for workers with caring responsibilities (Hantrais 2000). It remains, however, essentially a gender-blind concept applying equally to men and women, although there is a link to the gender equality agenda as work–life balance practices can serve the dual purpose of supporting women's participation in the labour market and at the same time facilitating a redistribution of caring responsibilities (largely unpaid) between men and women. Work–life balance policies and practices have become an integral part of EU employment policies and the Lisbon strategy for growth and employment expressly refers to the need for enabling 'people to stay in employment … by creating structures in which they can best combine their work and non work responsibilities' (European Foundation for the Improvement of Living & Working Conditions 2007, p. 3). Since then the concept has taken a particular turn, linking closely to stress experienced by those in paid employment, their ability to cope with the pressures of work and demands on their time and resources. In 2000 the UK's Labour government launched a major work–life balance campaign that focussed on the business case to highlight a number of benefits that employers could gain from the adoption of work–life balance practices: improved staff retention and recruitment, reduction of absenteeism, increased staff productivity and performance (Department of Trade & Industry 2001). There is some more recent evidence that measures taken to address the current economic crisis have widened inequalities, and that vulnerable demographic groups and organisations are bearing the brunt of national and international austerity measures (Leschke & Jepsen 2012; Pearson & Sweetman 2011).

The idea of work–life balance has relevance to those of us in the Western world who need to work to earn money to pay bills and who also want some kind of quality of life outside work. It is arguably not an issue for those for whom survival is the main focus of their lives, where enjoying leisure time is an unknown concept, or for whom work dominates to the exclusion of everything else such as refugees, subsistence farmers and indentured labourers. We also recognise that our disposition towards work–life balance changes over time as we age. The interest in work–life balance is in part driven by concerns that unbalanced work–family relationships can result in reduced health and performance outcomes for individuals, families and organisations. The term has developed over years with a move to encompass a broader scope: work–life balance includes employees who are not parents or carers, but who desire balance for non-work activities such as sports, study and travel. Work–life balance is one of the areas where the effect of austerity is most acutely felt. As a consequence many feel their balance out of kilter and it is important to register that men and women articulate their experience and struggle in different/gendered ways.

In their work, Kaliath and Brough (2008) have attempted to develop an agreed definition for the term to help ensure consistency in measurement and assist human resource management interventions in organisations. They argue that: '…without a direct measure of work–family balance, it is difficult to investigate the impact of 'family-friendly' policies on key individual and organisational outcome variables' (2008, p. 323). They review six conceptualisations of work–life balance found in the literature: multiple roles; equity across multiple roles; satisfaction between multiple roles; fulfilment of role salience between multiple roles; a relationship between conflict and facilitation; and perceived control between multiple roles. Based on their review they identify the two primary features of work–life balance and propose a new definition. The first thread of meaning they identify relates to 'perceptions of good balance' rather than 'conflict' or 'facilitation'. The second is the recognition that levels of change over time according to circumstances and specific life events. The definition they offer is:

> Work–life balance is the individual perception that work and non-work activities are compatible and promote growth in accordance with an individual's current life priorities (2008, p. 326).

According to Kaliath and Brough (2008), any assessment of work–life balance needs to include individual preferences in relation to current role, for example: whether an individual actually prefers to spend more or less time in work and non-work activities. Adopting the value base that it is in an individual's best interest to live a balanced life; they believe that effective balance leads to positive growth and development within both the work and/or non-work domains. Individual work/life priorities can voluntarily change to enable development in non-work activities: private study, new baby, extended travel and/or growth at work: such as working harder to gain formal work recognition and promotion.

Illustrating challenges of work–life balance through poetry

In 2015 in my capacity as a change management academic I was invited by the chief executive officer of a public sector organisation which had undergone a whole organisation restructuring to assist in helping staff come to terms with the change management process. All roles at middle management level and above had been redesigned and role holders were placed on redundancy notice, but also invited to apply for new roles. Some were successful, others left the organisation and others remained in new, but lower status roles. There was a large amount of upset and unhappiness throughout the organisation as a result of the changes and many were finding it difficult to adjust to the new order of things. One to one interviews were held with fifty new role holders, eight focus groups of up to 8 people were held for those who preferred to discuss the issues with others and a series of 6 voluntary workshops offered to anyone wishing to explore the personal impact of the changes further. The focus of the workshops varied according to the group and numbers attending varied from 12–24 participants. For two workshops the focus was on work–life balance, other workshops focused on surviving change and managing change differently. The idea of using arts-based approaches and specifically poetry was introduced with workshop briefing materials. Working with pictures and creating collages of experiences of change had been used as part of the individual interviews and participants were therefore aware of the benefits of taking a different and more experiential approach to working on emotive issues. The workshops lasted a day with four sessions: agreeing and relating to the workshop topic; creating poems; inquiring into the poems; reviewing learning and identifying actions. Exact timings and content varied according to the needs of the group. Poetry workshops were offered on a voluntary basis to anyone who wanted to explore and share their experiences further. They were offered as a way of helping to make sense of what was going on, to articulate the emotional experiences they has been through and to help come to terms with what had happened.

Selected abstracts follow of poems written during workshops that explore the experiences of work–life balance that were challenging workshop participants. The poems are reproduced with permission from participants; names and the organisation have been anonymised to protect confidentiality. Review discussions encouraged each participant to explore the imagery in their poem, the connections they made to it and the emotions that arose. Participants were also encouraged to explore how associations made to the poems might relate to their lives and what might need to change or improve for them if that seemed appropriate.

The following example is selected from one of the groups where experience of organisational change had left many feeling unhappy, disempowered and angry as is demonstrated in the emotive words and images used: 'big bad centre', 'beast', 'turmoil', 'like a sparrow at an insect' 'afraid', 'booted out'. In examining the imagery behind the words used, the group review setting enabled questioning about what could be done to change perceptions, behaviours and attitudes. In one workshop the group chose to focus on the word rhythm which occurred in a couple of places as a way of thinking about work–life balance: how the pace changes, flows and sets in well known tunes. There is a comfort in rhythm and the association made to life cycle, it can also be jarring if the music is not to your particular taste. In thinking about the organisational changes that participants had experienced a question about whether the changes were to individual taste or not was raised. This prompted a discussion about those who had done well out of the restructuring and those who felt they had lost out. The next area that caught the attention of the group was the mention of food and feasts, when the anticipation of a good meal is disappointed or greed takes over and you overindulge. This spoke to ambitious personal hopes that some had for the restructuring that were disappointed – the focus for resulting anger being placed on the 'big bad centre' and the 'beast'. Thoughts about the concept of work–life balance seemed to keep it as a largely unachievable thing in the realm of aspiration, torture, challenge, ideal and choice.

Collective poem: where each line is written by a different person	Key word prompt for next line
Work–life balance: a life time challenge	Challenge
The challenge is in the rhythm of life	Rhythm
Its rhythm depends on those around us	Depends
Whose balance depends on who?	Who
Who's afraid of the big bad centre	Afraid
Should I be afraid anymore?	
Work–life balance: a tortuous problem	Torture
A killer if you want to achieve everything	Killer
Choosing life is a killer – it might cost you work life to gain a life	
The cost of how you wish to live your life	Cost
Can we live with the demands that conflict within us?	Live
Conflict, conflab, congestion, indigestion	Conflict

Collective poem: where each line is written by a different person	Key word prompt for next line
Work–life balance: means time for lunch	Lunch
A moveable feast: an unsatisfactory meal	Feast
A feast if you get it, but a beast when you don't	Beast
If the beast is in the way then you have to change	Change
And rhythmically respond to change	Rhythmically
Rhythmically I complete my task and sleep	
Work–life balance: eluding my grasp	Grasp
Hold on to a sense of reality	Sense
'Nonsense' they told us	They
A group effort	Effort
If it's too much then it's too much – get a life	Life
But above all, life is for you to get	
Work–life balance: an ideal to aspire to	Ideal
The ideal slips away as the turmoil rages	Turmoil
The turmoil of the 25 h day	Day
Never a fulfilled day: never enough	Never
Never, never a question I ask myself whenever I don't achieve it	
Wherever, whenever, live life to the full	Whenever
Work–life balance: is a life choice	Choice
It's a question of choice for us all	Question
Like a sparrow at an insect	Like
But how does the balance feel when you clutch it?	Clutch
Taking the foot off the clutch is never easy	Foot
You often get booted out, if you have spent too long in the office	

Following on from the group poems an option for those interested and where there is time within the confines of the workshop is to unscramble the collective poem to discover the individual poem. In some ways it could be argued that the poems do not have the same flow or connectivity as the collective poems illustrated above as the key word prompt does not apply to help lead into the next line. Nevertheless the images created by the individual will hold significance for the author. These are the poems the individual did not know they had written.

For example, Keith's poem included the lines ' 'Nonsense' they told us', 'Taking the foot off the clutch is never easy' and 'Should I be afraid anymore?'. He was intrigued at how angry he was about being told 'nonsense' – it made him feel like a child being told off. The 'they' was senior management, who in his view were acting like critical parents and not listening to the experience of people in the organisation. He was also surprised by the way in his words, 'his best was not good enough', it didn't seem to matter how hard he worked it would never be enough, and this left him fearful for his career. In discussing the image of the clutch and shifting up a gear, (going for promotion) he came to think that his fear was more about fear of failure than putting in more work effort.

Allan found his poem difficult to unravel. He acknowledged that work wasn't everything for him and he was more interested in life outside work – 'A feast if you get it'. Being 'booted out' spoke to him of it being time to give up work and retire, rather than being told to go home because he had 'spent too long in the office'. This shows that the review sessions helped make sense of the meanings individuals ascribed to their poems, rather than someone else's interpretation which is important and helping shift understanding into reflexivity.

The next illustration is an example drawn from two women: Alice and Mary who worked together to create poems and then inquire into their meanings, and for whom the experience of work–life balance is at a critical point. The poems were written individually using key word prompts. The key word prompts are selected by the person writing the line of poetry, for example Mary writes ' Work life balance a never ending treadmill' and selects 'never ending' as the prompt for the next line.

Mary's poem	Key word prompt for next line
Work–life balance a never ending treadmill	Never ending
Never ending demands, decisions, things to do	Demands
I try so hard to respond and feel hopeless	Hopeless
I wish for positivity that hopeless can be turned into hope	Wish
No longer at your command, I am free	Free
To be free, I need to rest	

Mary is balancing her work with being primary carer for her husband who is severely mentally impaired following a stroke four years ago. Her physical and emotional exhaustion is reflected in her choice of 'treadmill' as the image for her work–life balance. In the one to one review session with Alice following the poetry writing she expressed how she felt trapped and unable to escape the drudgery of the demands on her. In her desire to be free, she recognises she needs a break and some rest. As someone who likes to look for the positives in life, Mary was surprised at how dark her poem was and how clearly it pointed to the need for her to have a break. In the review session she talked about how she might be able to get someone else to look after her husband while she had a holiday with friends using the Carer's support network that is available locally.

In the next poem Alice envisages herself as balancing scales, she discovers from her poem that the focus of work–life balance issues for her is work based, that she needs to find ways to delegate more and not take on so much of the emotional 'burden' from others that weighs her down. She was intrigued at the imagery of traipsing along muddy furrows – like a ploughing shire horse. She admired the strength of the horse, its loyalty and obedience, but could feel the weight of the mud sticking on her shoes and legs, making it hard to walk. She is also exhausted, but in a different way to Mary and she resolves to find more time for herself, and change her work practice.

Alice's poem	Key word prompt for next line
I am the scales, my arms are heavy…	Heavy
Heavy buckets of muck and filth, as I traipse along muddy furrows	Muck
Dirty, dirty, mess – exhausting clearing up behind others	
Others' anger and worry burden me and weigh me down	Others
Fair weights for all, share the load and the balance restores	Weigh
Find time to restore myself	Restores

These illustrations demonstrate how reflexive learning can be derived from collaborative writing. In the next section I will discuss how poetry and imagination combine into reflexivity through collaborative inquiry.

When working poetically with a topic such as work–life balance, rather than fix to a single definition it is important to allow random associations and meaning to emerge as this encourages a questioning of established definitions and give form to new understandings from an experiential base. Work–life balance as the topic for this inquiry contains within it a powerful and loaded metaphor. In addition, Greenhaus, Collins, and Shaw (2003) notice that sometimes the word 'balance' is used as a noun (when, for example, one is encouraged to achieve balance), and other times as a verb (to balance work and family demands) or an adjective (as in a balanced life) and that work–life balance often implies cutting back on work to spend more time with the family. It is questioning the focus on balance as positive, individual rather than shared balance, whether life changes are voluntary, (such as in unemployment or redundancy), or unforeseen, (such as illness and caring responsibilities for a partner or elderly parents), and that these can fall differently on men and women that becomes important in poetic inquiry.

Examining metaphor and visual imagination in work–life balance poetry

Visual imagination is stimulated in poetic writing not only through the use of metaphors and similes, but in the structure rhythm, rhyme pace and tone of the poem. The poems created through the 'corps exquis' method is given a flow in the use of connecting prompt words, which help to provide structure for collaborative writing processes. In the discussion that follows I will concentrate on the visual imagery used and connections made to it in terms of reflexive sense making. Lakoff and Johnson (2003) make the point that metaphor is typically viewed as characteristic of language alone, 'a matter of words rather than thought or action' they usefully add that metaphor is 'pervasive in everyday life, not just in language but in thought and action' (2003, p. 3) and therefore is an aid to reflexivity. The concepts and words we use structure what we perceive, the choices we make and how we function and relate to other people. Our conceptual system thus plays a central role in defining our everyday realities. The words we choose are therefore an important source of evidence for what the system we create and experience around us is like. Work–life balance has entered our understanding and has become what Lakoff and Johnson (2003) would categorise as a structural metaphor which:

> allow us to do more than just orient concepts, refer to them, quantify them etc. as we do with simple orientational and ontological metaphors; they allow us in addition, to use one highly structured and clearly delineated concept to structure another (2003, p. 61).

The poems produced therefore need to be understood in terms of both the experiential, contextual and cultural basis, with a reflexive understanding that the meanings derived are relevant at a point in time and therefore not permanent.

Kaliath and Brough's (2008) review of different conceptualisations of work–life balance focussed on the issue of roles and multiple roles, satisfaction, fulfilment and salience between different roles. When investigating the concept from a metaphorical and poetic perspective based on lived experience, the incommensurability of achieving a permanent balance becomes evident. Probably the first thought about work–life balance in terms of imagery draws attention to the situational notion of balance. The value base behind this is that to be balanced is positive; a good healthy thing to have where there is therefore no conflict of interests between different roles and the individual is in control of their life and work. On the other hand, to be unbalanced, either physically or mentally is viewed as bad, lacking. When balanced we are functioning human beings, sane, in control of our emotions, and physical self; whereas to be unbalanced has a sense of mental or physical ill health, lack of control, excess and greed and we are out of control of ourselves and our surroundings. This is where the rub lies: for to acknowledge that somehow work–life balance has not been or cannot be achieved results in a sense of deficit and a permanently deficient model for living life. Indeed the collective poems show how the ideal of work–life balance is experienced as an impossible goal.

> ...an ideal to aspire to
> The ideal slips away as the turmoil rages
> The turmoil of the 25 h day...

When thinking of balance and scales the image of fairness and justice is introduced. Whatever is loaded on one side, whether heavy or light, needs exactly equal measure on the other side. Its meaning is therefore also ontological in the sense that balance is a bounded concept, Whatever is balanced, whether it is time, money, physical effort, emotional investment etc. needs to be matched in a way that the individual feels is fair and just. This means that to achieve balance there needs to be stillness and stability and that must hold. We can think of Olympic gymnasts perfectly poised and balanced holding a difficult position and defying gravity, however this can only be maintained for a very short time and the training, skills development, aptitude, daring, courage and strength to hold these poses is considerable – not accessible or obtainable for most of us. This state is difficult to achieve and impossible to maintain as nothing in life is static. As dynamic sentient human beings we are always changing, physically and mentally: growing older, making choices etc. and the notion of maintaining a single state in work–life balance is therefore irrelevant. We also are unable to control and fully influence our surroundings and events that take place around us either in the work place or at home as Mary and Alice's poems aptly illustrated:

> Never ending demands, decisions, things to do
> I try so hard to respond and feel hopeless

and

> Others' anger and worry burden me and weigh me down

What then is being balanced in work–life balance in addition to the obvious answer: work and life? Time weighed against money is one possibility as a way of tackling the dilemma of whether we work to live or live to work. Maximising one is supposed to facilitate the other. However this is another problematic duality as time is a fixed and finite resource, whereas money is not. The following excerpt from the collective poem illustrates this well:

Choosing life is a killer – it might cost you work life to gain a life
The cost of how you wish to live your life

Lakoff and Johnson (2003, p. 9) talk about the underlying metaphorical concepts to time and money and how viewing time and money as limited and valuable resource is specifically tied to our industrial society, influencing how we think about and act upon experiences of the balance between the two concepts. In addition labour and time are described as material resources serving purposeful ends; they can be quantified and given value, used up progressively as the purpose is served (2003, p. 65):

A feast if you get it, but a beast when you don't
...
Never a fulfilled day: never enough

According to Lakoff and Johnson the metaphor of labour as a kind of activity assumes a clear distinction with those things that are not labour:

It makes the assumption that we can tell work from play and productive activity from non-productive activity. These assumptions obviously fail to fit reality much of the time, except perhaps on assembly lines, chain gangs etc. The view of labour as merely a kind of activity, independent of who performs it, how he experiences it and what it means in his life, hides the issues of whether the work is personally meaningful, satisfying and humane (2003, p. 67).

Perhaps that is what our participants are saying about their work–life balance in that they do not feel their work is meaningful, satisfying and humane? We can see the range of negative associations that those writing about their experiences have identified:

a treadmill
buckets of muck and filth
a killer
a moveable feast
turmoil
a tortuous problem
a sparrow pecking at an insect

These emphasise how difficult achieving a positive work–life balance is for many and I am reminded that the participants' poems represented in this article are from a group who are all in their late 50's and arguably are facing different emerging priorities at this stage in their lives – thinking about retirement and wanting to develop other interests beyond work demands and at the same time outside work caring responsibilities shift from children to partners and parents. The imagery in poetry draws focus to some and away from other possibilities, as Cunliffe (2003) points out:

...meaning is created through a constant interplay of presence/absence and what is not said is as important as what is said because each supplements the other ... actively exploring the paradoxical relationship between presence and absence ... reveals contradictions in truth claims and the instability of language by turning meaning back on itself (2003, p. 987).

In seeking out more positive alternatives to counterbalance the negativity in the poems, I noticed the reference to 'rhythm of life' and 'rhythmically' which offers a more accepting and holistic possibility for coping with the challenges that come with trying to achieve a positive work–life balance. Daring 'to take the foot off the clutch' and presumably freewheel holds a similar sense of acceptance. The following collaborative poem illustrates the fluidity participants at another workshop felt is important when thinking about and working with a concept such as work–life balance. This group were unhappy with the images of work–life balance as scales and balance and worked together to find something that was more fluid and elemental to describe their life challenges. The ebb and flow of water seemed to offer different possibilities:

> Work life balance is like fighting against a strong tide
> With rocks opposite each other and crashing waves
> Relentlessly eroding each into separate grains of sand
> The impossibility of separate lives as work floods in
> Stop! The waves encroach
> Think, think – do you want this?

Conclusion

This paper has explored imagination and reflexivity by focusing upon the creation of collaboratively generated poems, together with action inquiry as an enabler of reflexive practice, exploring how this process supports personal and professional development in relation to the issue of work–life balance. I have demonstrated that there is a power in poetry to help inquire into and illuminate new understandings based on lived experiences which is demonstrated in the creative and imaginative use of imagery contained within the choice of words and the connections made to them. The focus for this work has been on the challenges to understand work–life balance from an experiential perspective and has provided a different way of thinking about and working with the concept. Despite government legislation and arguments set out for employers for the business case of work–life balance, the poems illustrate how it is experienced as a largely unattainable goal and as a consequence leaves people feeling dissatisfied and with a sense of failure, particularly at later stages in working life. I have also found that writing poetry helps an individual understand where their focus of attention has been placed and encourages reflexivity in thinking through alternative conceptualisations and actions that might produce benefits for individuals, their families and the organisations they work for. My personal reflection on the poetic inquiry process with reflexive analysis of meaning and action derived from the poems suggests that this is an area that merits further development.

References

Cunliffe, A. L. (2003). Reflexive inquiry in organizational research: questions and possibilities. *Human Relations, 56*, 983–1003.

Darmer, P., & Grisoni, L. (Eds.). (2011). The opportunity of poetry: Pursuing the liberty of poetics and poetry in organizing, leading and managing. *Tamara, 9*, 5–13.

Department of Trade and Industry. (2001). *The Business case*. London: Department of Trade and Industry.

Ellis, J., & Kiely, J. (2000, June). Action inquiry strategies: Taking stock and moving forward. *Journal of Applied Management Studies, 9*, 83–94.

European Foundation for the Improvement of Living and Working Conditions. 2007. Work-life balance: Solving the dilemma. Retrieved from http://www.eurofound.europa.eu?publications/htmlfiles/ef0789.htm

Greenhaus, J. H., Collins, K. M., & Shaw, J. D. (2003). The relation between work – family balance and quality of life. *Journal of Vocational Behavior, 63*, 510–531.

Grisoni, L. (2008). Poetry. In M. Broussine (Ed.), *Creative methods in organizational research* (Chap. 7, pp. 108–127). London: Sage.

Grisoni, L.. 2009. Flavouring organisational learning with poetry. In J. Kociatkjewicsz, & D. Jemelniak (Eds.), *Handbook of research on knowledge intensive organisations* (pp. 98–115). San Francisco, CA: IGI Global.

Grisoni, L., & Kirk, P. (2006). Verse, voice and va va voom!: Illuminating management processes through poetry. *Management Decision, 44*, 512–525.

Hantrais, L. (2000). *Social policy in the European Union*. London: Macmillan.

Kaliath, T., & Brough, P. (2008). Work–life balance: A review of the meaning of the balance construct. *Journal of Management & Organization, 14*, 323–327.

Knowles, J. G., & Cole, A. L. (2008). *Handbook of the arts in qualitative research: Perspectives, methodologies, examples, and issues*. London: Sage.

Lafreniere, D., & Cox, S. M. (2012). 'If you can call it a poem': Toward a framework for the assessment of arts-based works. *Qualitative Research, 13*, 318–336.

Lakoff, G., & Johnson, M. (2003). *Metaphors we live by*. Chicago, IL: University of Chicago Press.

Leschke, J., & Jepsen, M. (2012). Introduction: Crisis, policy responses and widening inequalities in the EU. *International Labour Review, 151*, 289.

Morgan, C., Lange, K., & Buswick, T. (2010). *What poetry brings to business*. Ann Arbor, MI: Michigan Press.

Page, M., Grisoni, L., & Turner, A. (2014). Dreaming fairness and re-imagining equality and diversity through participative aesthetic inquiry. *Management Learning., 45*, 577–592.

Pearson, R., & Sweetman, C. (Eds.). (2011). *Gender and the economic crisis*. Oxford: Practical Action Publishing.

Siegesmund, R., Cahnmann-Taylor, M. (2008). The tensions of arts-based research in education reconsidered: the promise for practice. In M. Canhnmann-Taylor & R. Siegesmund (Eds.), *Arts-based research in education: Foundations for practice* (pp. 231–246). New York, NY: Routledge.

Torbert, W. (2004). *Action inquiry: The secret of timely and transforming leadership*. San Fransisco, CA: Berrett-Koehler.

Whyte, D. (1994). *The Heart aroused: Poetry and the preservation of the soul in Corporate America*. New York, NY: Double Day Press.

From the associative use of visual imagery in organisational contexts, described by Grisoni, we pass from a practice focused method to another method that also uses associative visual thinking and that was originally developed for exploratory research-based inquiry in the field of public art. The aim of the visual matrix was to enable people to express their experience of art through images and affect - without it becoming overwhelmed by words. It was devised in order to help people who are not specialists in art to articulate artistic experience that they found difficult to put into words. It is now being applied to highly sensitive subjects, or subjects that are emotionally hard to grasp, and which people also find it difficult to speak of.

Discourses of positive and active aging are now widespread throughout the Western World and are promoted by organisations that advocate for needs of older people. They tend to overwhelm the difficult emotions with accompany life transitions – rendering them unspeakable. The underlying assumption appears to be that only by remaining active and independent can older people be valued as citizens with the capacity to live, spend, consume and provide practical care and emotional labour. As retirement ages rise there will also be increasing expectations that they participate in the work-force.

However desirable this prospect might appear to some, there is the potential for it to be experienced by those in poor health, and approaching death, as a disavowal of vulnerability - a necessary aspect of the human condition to which we all eventually succumb. As the authors point out the positivity of active ageing can perversely make the experience of dependency hard to speak of, hard to think about, and hard bear. In the face of their own aging and sooner or later their dying, researchers in this field are themselves easily captured by the manic hopefulness of these discourses. How then can thay make space for the more difficult emotions that the vulnerabilities of old age arouse?

Visual matrix methodology is led by imagery and affect, rather than discursive language. The pilot project discussed in this paper engaged three groups – of various ages - on the subject of transitions of old age: work-life to retirement, mental health to dementia, and life to death. By working with imagery stimulated by these transitions, these groups were able contain anxieties which they would normally have found very difficult to acknowledge and which tend to be split off and 'banished' from awareness. Instead they were able to emotionally resolve some of their fears of aging and dying integrating them with a realistic hopefulness to be found in the generations, in eternal cycles of death and re-birth, and in relationship to nature.

The visual matrix, developed out of 'social dreaming' originally as a research method. It is clearly a tool of engagement in its own right. This article shows that it has potential use in residential settings, and among staff working with older people (and indeed among other groups in contexts where anxiety impedes thought). It offers the possibility of new modes of communication and authentic self-expression that could support compassionate care.

Anne Liveng, Ellen Ramvi, Lynn Froggett, Julian Manley, Wendy Hollway, Ase Lading and Birgitta H. Gripsrud

IMAGINING TRANSITIONS IN OLD AGE THROUGH THE VISUAL MATRIX METHOD: THINKING ABOUT WHAT IS HARD TO BEAR

Dominant discourses of ageing are often confined to what is less painful to think about and therefore idealise or denigrate ageing and later life. We present findings from an exploratory psychosocial study, in a Nordic context, into three later-life transitions: from working life to retirement, from mental health to dementia and from life to death. Because, for some, these topics are hard to bear and therefore defended against and routinely excluded from everyday awareness, we used a method led by imagery and affect — the Visual Matrix — to elicit participants' free associative personal and collective imagination. Through analysis of data extracts, on the three transitions, we illustrate oscillations between defending against the challenges of ageing and realism in facing the anxieties it can provoke. A recurring theme includes the finality of individual life and the inter-generational continuity, which together link life and death, hope and despair, separation and connectedness.

Introduction: the challenges of ageing

This article is based on an interdisciplinary research project, *Exploring Life Transitions in Old Age through a Visual Matrix* (2014–15) which used a group-based, image-led research method in a Nordic setting involving health professionals and academics. Our aim was to explore the transferability of the method to the psychosocial challenges of ageing and to discover what a methodology based on imagery, affect and visualisation might yield – particularly in relation to those aspects of ageing which are notoriously hard to speak of and for many, including ourselves, hard to imagine and hard to bear.[1] For this purpose we held three two-day visual matrix workshops, one in Norway and two in Denmark, one for each of three thematic transitions: from working life to retirement, from mental health to dementia and from life to death. This was also a 'self-research' project insofar as funding was to trial the Visual Matrix method with ourselves as primary participants, along with a number of others who had a personal or professional interest in the topic. Whilst the core group (the authors of this article) was constant across the three workshops, invited externals varied. The numbers also varied between ten and twenty, with one workshop (on the transition to dementia) involving a group of women who held professional, advocacy or caring roles in the field. Ages ranged from mid-thirties to mid-sixties, so some of us felt close to the transitions we were investigating.

In common with most other western societies, Nordic countries face the challenge of coping with ageing populations while responding to demands that welfare states should cut costs. Questions such as how people age, postponing functional decline connected to ageing, who should pay for services and who should have responsibility for health and care have become pressing political issues. Nordic, former social democratic, welfare state regimes (Esping-Andersen & Andersen 1990) have responded to the economic and demographic challenges with changes in attitudes and policies. The political ethos framing care now emphasises efficiency (Wrede 2008) while responsibility for minimising what is articulated as an economic burden falls increasingly on the elderly themselves (Kamp & Hvid 2012). As in other high income countries policy and conventional discourse co-create a binary interpretation of later life as *either* marked by good health, resources and free-time activities *or* by decline and illness (Grenier 2012). Policy documents highlight how older adults can make their own choices and live active, meaningful, healthy lives. Such policies put an emphasis on the wish of older adults to be autonomous in the sense of not being dependent on help from others (Dahl 2011; Liveng 2016). In Denmark older generations have been constructed as an economic burden leading to higher retirement age (65 years old at present rising to 68 in 2030).[2] In media discourses on the other hand the financially resourceful older generations are labelled 'grey gold' due to their consumer capabilities and advertisements are increasingly directed at the retirement population.

When approaching *transitions from working life to retirement* from a psychosocial perspective, we ask whether and how this media, policy and research focus on 'active ageing' is reflected in visualisations of the transition. How, for example, does this frame of reference produce a reassessment of subjective identities of ageing people (Dahl & Rasmussen 2012; Holstein & Minkler 2003)? How do older adults cope with the uncertainties connected to retirement as a new and unknown phase of life (Moffatt & Heaven 2016)? What is imagined and experienced, given that retirement is often associated with loss and can involve major changes in identity (Fristrup & Munksgaard 2009; Goodwin & O'Connor 2012)? Statistical data illustrate that retirement potentially threatens mental health, as evidenced in the substantial increase in antidepressant use among Danish women between the ages of 60–64 and continuing into old age (Jørgensen 2012). At the same time, retirement is endowed with hopeful expectations for a new 'third age', which for many in the Nordic context is a phase of life with relatively good health, consumer opportunities and work-free time (Etwil, Sørensen, & Mackie 2011).

Our second theme, *the transition from usual mental functioning to dementia*, arouses anxiety at the prospect and reality of living with dementia and poses complex challenges. Dementia is a broad category of brain diseases that cause long term and often gradual decline in the ability to think, act and remember. The number of sufferers will increase in future years as the generations born after the Second World War get older (Prince et al. 2015). More people will be concerned with the illness, as patients, carers (professional and informal) or relatives (Andersen-Ranberg, Birk-Olsen, Kronborg Andersen, Christiansen, & Strid 2007; Evans & Lee 2014). Dementia is mostly seen from an illness and care perspective, and how the spread of the disease affects people who are not directly involved with the illness is not a focus. A discourse imbued with fear is often used – for example *The Danish Dementia Alliance* writes in a vision paper, 'Dementia is a harsh, deadly disease. Suddenly one day – and then relentlessly day-by-day – it evaporates your life. Bit by bit. Slowly at first, then faster, but always certain. Your memory, your past, present and future, your sense of time and space – your self – disappear in the end into a big black hole. (…) Dementia is not just a disease that takes our lives. It is a disease that takes life away while living' (Demensalliancen 2015, p. 4).³ As a response to representations such as this *The Canadian Partnerships in Dementia Care Alliance* have criticised 'the tragedy discourse that surrounds dementia' (Canadian Partnerships in Dementia Care Alliance 2015).

Unsurprisingly, these discourses affect people diagnosed with the disease who struggle with understanding themselves in the context of stigmatising labelling – 'the dreadful names' (Langdon, Eagle, & Warner 2007). They also affect older people in general, as age is an important factor in developing the disease (Corner & Bond 2004). Behuniak (2011) has argued that the construction of people suffering from Alzheimer's disease as 'living dead' or 'zombies' is highly problematic, as it leads to stigmatisation and a dehumanisation based on disgust and terror. In her view representations of dementia are relevant to every generation (ibid. p. 72): people suffering from the disease are constructed as 'other' and negative emotional responses among the 'healthy' are fuelled. Less attention is paid to how these discourses tap into, and are produced and reproduced by, the embodied experiences of ageing that are the baseline for individuals' meaning-making and acting: resilient, fearful, perhaps paranoid, perhaps realistic.

Our third theme, *the transition from life to death* is often neglected in secular cultures (Jacobsen 2010). End of life care has historically moved from containment in the home to treatment in hospitals and care institutions (Kaasa 2008). Research suggests, however, that a person's gradual encounter with death can provide a new and possibly enhanced awareness and understanding of self (Molzahn 2007; Yalom 2008). In their literature review of the end of life in old age, with a particular focus on cultural concerns, Lloyd, White, and Sutton (2010) identified a bias towards end-of-life care and treatment decisions, rather than older people's experiences of end of life more generally. They also identified a clear message across the entire corpus of review material that a better understanding is needed of ethnic and cultural differences in beliefs and practices as people approach death in old age. In several studies participants expressed a fear of loss of dignity and increased dependency as well as anxieties regarding symptoms of old age and being a burden to others. Pleschberger (2007) found fear of being a burden a major theme among older adults, and argued that this fear 'cannot be separated from the broader cultural and societal values expressed in daily reminders about the cost of caring for dependent old people' (Pleschberger 2007, p. 201).

In general, there is an inconsistency between the daily reminders to which we are exposed and an apparent silence. Österlind, Hansebo, Andersson, and Ternestedt (2011) showed in a study of the discourses of death and dying that death was silenced even among staff in nursing homes: 'Death was held at bay, and the emotions experienced by the staff when an old person died were ignored' (2011, p. 538). Also among nurses in home care this silence is paramount (Aadland & Ramvi, 2016). Österlind et al. (2011) relate their findings to another prevailing split discourse about independence as the most positive human quality, and dependency and frailty as the most feared. This study also highlights the 'need for a change in the content and scope of care for older people in a way that visualises dying as a process requiring attention before the moment of death' (ibid. p. 540). They advocate an alternative discourse where death is not made invisible, and where life at the same time opens up to the reality of death and the feelings connected to it.

Transitions can be seen as an inevitable and continuous part of human life, occasioning social, physical and cultural changes. These are accompanied by emotional challenges in the form of new positions, resources, statuses and capacities, which can be understood as connected to both socially constructed meanings of the transitions, physical changes and psycho-biographically created expectations of the transition (Chodorow 1999; Erikson & Erikson 1998; Grenier 2012). Individuals will therefore experience these differently according to geographical, social and personal/biographical contexts.

Implications for methodology: using the Visual Matrix to generate and analyse free associative visual data

If changes are hard to face, and if these difficulties are also reflected at the sociocultural and discursive level, they also constitute challenges for research, because painful, frustrating, even unbearable ideas are most easily defended against through not thinking about them: in common parlance, we say 'I can't bear to think about that'. If a research participant cannot think about it, then a standard interview-based research method is likely to generate sanitised accounts rather than data that give insight into the more painful aspects of experiences of ageing (Hollway 2015). Given the nature of the material we were dealing with in this study, we needed a psychosocial method which could accommodate anxieties arising from individual experience of research participants while understanding their expression (or lack of it) in sociocultural terms. We needed to reflexively make use of our own subjective experience whilst questioning socially constructed ideas of these transitions which, when combined with personal and subjective fears of old age, arouse shared anxieties. Such anxieties are reproduced and transmitted through social processes of which we are at times unaware, and against which we habitually defend ourselves (Hollway & Jefferson 2013).

The way in which old age is imagined, feared, or celebrated is key to a psychosocial understanding of these transitions as well as the material difficulties they pose. Our research settings therefore needed to be sufficiently contained to accommodate the anxieties aroused by the subject matter and to register the affect of the participant group as a whole. At the same time they had to make space for personal emotions of grief, sadness, anger and despair that were likely to appear alongside hopefulness and compassion. Our approach therefore required a process sufficiently sensitive to the nuances of feeling among participants, enabling them to think and feel in the face of the difficulty of the subject matter.

A number of features of the visual matrix method made it suitable for our purpose. Firstly, it elicits images, affects and ideas aroused by a visual stimulus that acts on individual participants, but it does so in a group setting that reveals the sociocultural significance of shared responses. Secondly, it enables expression of what might otherwise be difficult to articulate and hence offers the possibility of researching 'beneath the surface' of awareness. Thirdly, by facilitating associations, rather than analysis or argumentation, it creates the conditions for an emergent process[4] whereby thoughts are symbolised imagistically and are imbued with affect. What emerges is manifest in the here-and-now of the matrix rather than explained after the event; participants are asked not what they *think* about the object of inquiry, but what they *feel* and *visualise*. Fourthly, it creates a container[5] allowing difficult material to be thought about in a setting, and with a facilitation technique, that feels safe and respectful; from an ethical perspective it has its own 'built-in' de-brief in the form of the post-matrix discussion. Fifthly, participants themselves establish the frame for analysis in the post-matrix discussion, thereby informing the later interpretative work of the research team.

Each of the visual matrices was preceded by a brief session in which people were invited to draw for themselves whatever the topic of the matrix suggested. If they wished, they could share this with the rest of the group. Then, as is usual for a visual matrix, they were seated in a 'snowflake' formation that encourages people to speak to a shared space rather than to one another. Rather than direct questioning according to topic guides, they were invited to offer their images, associations and feelings, if they wished and as and when they occurred.[6]

Over the course of the sessions (each lasting up to an hour), images accumulated as participants responded to the topic and to the visualisations presented by others. This generated 'collages' of affect-laden imagery. Images arose out of personal experience, but because they prompted associated images and ideas in others who elaborated and transformed them, the matrix took on a shared and interwoven character. After this, participants reconvened, seated around a board or flipchart, to participate in an image mapping session – the post matrix discussion – which identifies intensities of affect, dense clusters of imagery, inter-connections between ideas and strands of thought. The visual matrix and the post matrix discussion were audio-recorded, transcribed and made available for further interpretation by the research team.[7]

Ageing, splitting and the visual matrix as container

With reference to the work of Bion (1970) we can conceive of the facilitation as establishing the parameters of the matrix and containing the process in order to allay anxiety so that participants can work creatively with the imagery and affect that emerge. When functioning optimally the matrix operates in and through a state of 'reverie', a meditative form of mental 'metabolism' in which freely flowing images, thoughts and ideas can be contained and processed. At such times, what is known and yet unthinkable can be thought and shared. As it proceeds, the containment and reverie of the matrix help to attenuate dualities of thought and feeling among participants by allowing split thoughts and opposing ideas to co-exist in the here-and-now of the matrix, without foreclosure. Overlaying images, affects, thoughts and feelings accumulate as the continuous movement and interweaving of imagery proceeds, so that many inter-connecting ideas can be linked, rather than remaining as split positions, destructive of the thinking process.

The likelihood of splitting in relation to the anxieties that accompany the idea of ageing is illuminated through a Kleinian conceptual framework that proved to be useful in making sense of the data. Kleinian psychoanalytic theory (Klein 1975), contrasts two modes of experiencing, paranoid-schizoid and depressive. The paranoid-schizoid position, developmentally the earlier mode, recurs and alternates with depressive states of mind throughout life. Whilst operating in this mode, bad elements of experiences are split off from good, more welcome ones. To rid oneself of the discomfort, these hard-to-bear elements (here, for example, the losses of retirement; the possibility of dementia in ourselves or our loved ones; the inevitability of death) are projected onto external objects, while the good elements are retained as belonging to the inner world of the psyche. The splitting of good and bad elements is captured by the concept of 'schizoid', while the concept of 'paranoid' derives from the consequent feeling that bad features, now located in the external world, threaten a person's psychic safety. Such defence mechanisms are commonplace ways of creating a liveable and orderly life, but when a paranoid-schizoid state of mind predominates, it entails not being able to reflect realistically on the prospect of ageing. It is therefore likely that such states of mind will oscillate with the depressive mode of experiencing in which good and bad are accepted within a realistic ambivalence. The ability to withstand paranoid-schizoid anxiety and integrate experience depends on the activation of psychic containers enabled by a setting where seeming oppositions can be safely held in mind and the complexity of experience apprehended. A well-functioning visual matrix offers just such a setting, enabling images and ideas from many different sources to co-exist, sometimes in tension, in a shared space. The interweaving of images and associations as the matrixial collage accumulates tends to generate richly multi-faceted data that can be owned by the participants as a whole. Through the presentation of imagery, participants can respond imaginatively to hard-to-bear topics, allowing a degree of integration of thought and feeling. This generates data which can be interpreted in depth by the research team working as a panel. Data are analysed in terms of content (what was presented); performative qualities (how it was presented) and for its unstated, partly unconscious and sociocultural significance (why it was said in the way that it was) (Hollway & Volmerg 2010).

Finding patterns in data produced from three visual matrices

It was striking how the dual, seemingly split, nature of discourses regarding ageing was reproduced through thematic and affective oscillations in the course of the matrix:

- Life – death
- Trans-generational continuity – the finality of individual life
- Relatedness of friendship and family – loss, separation and isolation
- Holding on to life – giving up
- Hope – despair
- Suffering – pleasure
- Health – impairment
- Sense-making and control – hopelessness and powerlessness
- Impotence in the face of natural forces – harmony with nature
- Blankness – the capacity to think about the transitions in old age.

These apparent dualities arose through a process of shared imagining, reflecting their sociocultural significance as well as existential resonance for individual participants. However, rather than reproducing an either-or (split) mode of thinking, they were often dynamically and ambivalently inter-related through oscillations in the visual imaginary of the transitions, replete with their emotional content, reworked throughout the matrix. We illustrate this movement between split off (paranoid-schizoid) and integrated (depressive) modes of thought below.

Transitions from working life to retirement

The transitional stage from working life to retirement represents the threshold to old age. On the one hand retirement is visualised in the matrix through polarised images and comments, reflecting popular ideas of older people as healthy, wealthy and realising their potentials; or as part of an 'elderly tsunami' consisting of a mass of look-alikes without individuality and sexuality. On the other hand the matrix includes elaborated and nuanced images, which contradict any easily formulated idea of what it means to be retired and old. Especially interesting are the recurring images of relationships among generations, which stand in opposition to predominant cultural ideals of independence and the ambivalent fearing and longing for 'giving in/giving up' – becoming passive, slow, inactive – a surrender to the dimensions of old age, which in the prevailing activity discourse has been suppressed.

The complex affect behind these themes of transition was expressed through a recurring image of an ageing tree, which in its most condensed form was brought into the matrix as a handkerchief tree. This cropped up towards the end of the matrix and seems to integrate many of the prior images and reflections. These included the following images of trees:

- A thick oak, with heavy branches, no leaves but a single red berry.
- An apple tree – its fruit sweetening at nature's rather than humans' pace.
- The Tree of Knowledge, associating to loss of innocence, and retirement as a possibility to win back innocence and spontaneity.
- A tree rotten in the middle, but still growing.
- A mysterious oak tree planted by King Christian IV, shaped by the west wind.
- A bonsai tree, growing slowly, pruned with nail scissors.
- A handkerchief tree that takes ten years until it fully matures.
- A pine tree planted by a grandfather, deformed by wind.

Of these, we have chosen to analyse the following extract of the image of the handkerchief tree from the transcript of the visual matrix:

I have a sister; ten years younger than I am. When she turned 55 in December I started trying to grow a handkerchief tree. It takes 1–2 years before you can see a small tiny green top. It takes 10 years before it's a tree. So I gave it to her and said that I'm looking forward to seeing her garden, when I'm turning 75 – enjoying the handkerchief tree – and with that I want to tell: I remember when I was a child I loved lying in the grass seeing the laundry, [...] blowing in the wind.

The handkerchief tree grows simultaneously with the transition of first, older, sister and then the second, younger one from working life to retirement; its maturing traces the 10-year age gap between the two. As a gift it confirms and enhances the relationship between the two sisters, and as a birthday present it connects childhood with the present age of the sisters. With its slow rate of maturing it holds the promise of fertility and points to their potential future: the expectation of being able to enjoy this tree as old women, sitting in the garden. Symbolically the gift communicates the wish of the older sister to be alive and together with the younger sister in old age, as they were in childhood. In a folding of time, the tree's 'handkerchiefs' draw in a sensuous childhood memory of harmony through the image of lying in the grass, looking at clean laundry. From a mode of doing (growing the tree, giving the gift) the image changes to represent a mode of being (lying, looking, enjoying), which provides pleasure in the present moment, reflecting the innocence inherent in the former tree images At the same time this pleasure is tainted with a possible sadness through the handkerchiefs which potentially associate to weeping. The mode of being in this image is not equivalent to passivity, but represents presence and awareness in the present moment.

Together with the handkerchief tree, the other images of trees in the matrix represent continuity, life as something which transgresses the limitations of the single individual, slow growth, survival in adversity, tenacity and intergenerational bonds. As in Nordic cultural tradition, the tree in the matrix symbolises life, represented in mythology through the tree Yggdrasill.[8] In Christianity, the Tree of Knowledge bears tempting fruits. In the matrix trees are presented as natural creations with their own life-course, shaped by their surroundings. The tree image integrates a sadness emerging through references to decay (only one single berry, rotten in the middle) and being at the mercy of natural forces beyond human control (deformed by the wind) with trust in regeneration and slow growth. The tree confronts us with the finality of individual life while also offering consolation through natural continuity, linked to generational continuity. In this way, the harmonious character of the tree image signifies an integrative, primarily depressive, mode of relating to ageing; an acceptance of the limitation of personal life as well as the mourning this implies, together with a trust in connection and hope linked to the continuation of life through the past and coming generations.

The visual matrix on transitions from normal mental ability to dementia

The matrix on dementia reflected the idea of the person suffering from dementia as 'disappearing' – imagined in the matrix, for instance as looking in the mirror, expecting to see oneself and actually seeing a ghost. The idea of disappearing was further elaborated by becoming associated to the disappearance of sand in the image of the hourglass. Below, we analyse this image, its development and the oscillations it included.

In the transcript, the first mention of this image is 'I see an hourglass with sand. It's not only running out through the bottom; there's a hole and the sand is disappearing'. In what follows it is as if such hopelessness is initially too much to bear, and so the matrix continues with attempts to find alternatives: noise, anger, fear, escape, the body as opposed to the mind and the fulfilment of a family doing its best for a member with dementia. Eventually, the hourglass image is picked up again and developed, leading this time to images of acceptance and mourning. The passage moves between paranoid-schizoid modes of experience to a depressive facing of the losses and rewards involved in dementia:

> The image of the hourglass and the sand was, eh – the hole in the bottom of the hourglass stayed with me, and brings to my mind the image of that sand falling into a huge desert, like the Sahara desert, where there's plenty of sand, but nothing else. And, eh, imagining someone in the middle of that desert and nothing there, but sand, lots of sand.

The hourglass incorporates two contrasting transitions: the undamaged hourglass and then the hourglass with a hole in the bottom. The first represents the hope that our lives will run in the expected fashion, leading to a death that, while its reality cannot be denied, can be contained within a normal life cycle, like the sand in an undamaged hourglass. This idea is threatened by the hole in the hourglass that represents an ageing that seeps away through loss of a sense of self prior to death.

An attempt to escape from the starkness of this image follows, with an appeal to an earlier image of stardust to introduce beauty into the desert sky along with the emptiness: 'still it's full [of stars] in the desert'. This allows something positive to be sought from dementia: 'I can feel the happiness as an old woman'. The othering of the demented ('not me') is strikingly changed in this image as the speaker imagines 'remembering the exact words I thought were out of my mind'. The next speaker shifts back to the position of the other by remembering her grandmother. From here she is facing a loved one's death at a remove of two generations. From this position, using the star image, she introduces the possibility of connection after death, remembering her grandmother telling her that 'I could look upon a star and think of her and she would send me nice thoughts when she was not here any longer'. In this image, the loss involved in another's death – the bad element – is optimistically banished in favour of the reassuring idea that we never fully lose our loved ones.

The participants in the matrix then make an associative leap, moving away from the stardust and back to the darkness of the hole in the hourglass. In the next image, the hole in the hourglass becomes linked to the image of rabbit holes on a 'steep slope', maybe the slippery slope of dementia. The rabbit holes of this image seem analogous to the pitted holes in a brain of a person suffering from dementia. Probably because the idea of this pitted mind is almost unbearable 'I found myself drawing a rabbit, but while I was drawing it, it morphed into a hare'. The image can thus represent contrasting qualities: the rabbit burrowing, out of sight, creating more and more holes; the hare providing escape, 'running into the distance somewhere'.

The visual matrix on transitions from life to death

Images produced in this matrix were very diverse; the theme of death was associated with strong feelings of fear, anger, guilt, sadness, fascination and wonder. The opening intervention 'I can't imagine myself dying or as a dead person' reflected the emotional undercurrent of the session as a whole – death is almost unimaginable, whether your own death, a child's, a suicide, death caused by an accident or even by old age. One participant said that she hated it when the curtains closed in the crematorium, thereby expressing fear of both the final separation from someone and the mystery of death: what happens behind the curtains? Another one recalled words on a gravestone: 'Where you stay, I stayed before'. Dying is a shared fate, but the inscription on the grave may still feel as if it does not concern the person who reads it. The socially formulated *big divide* between life and death makes our shared fate almost unthinkable.

Participants showed their love and their aggression in narratives or images where dying or dead animals and pets were involved. Children dying, or in danger of death, were associated with strong guilt because of the parents' lack of attention or failure to provide protection. Suicide was mentioned twice. 'I felt that maybe it is better to die', one participant said about a difficult period in her life, but it was received with silence as an indication of its content being taboo or too painful to imagine for the matrix. Still, the legalised and frightening power to end a life cropped up in a narrated scene from a hospital where the health care personnel wanted to stop giving the participant's mother water through the veins, but the participant hated the gruesome idea of allowing her 'mother to [die of] thirst'.

Although religion as a containing frame for the mystery of death was not pervasive, Christian imagery emerged: for example, a Pietà sculpture of the grieving Madonna with her dead child on her lap and the cross presented as an ambiguous symbol of Christ. The idea of a graveyard appeared more comforting as a place symbolising a shared destiny across the generations.

In all these images, death was imagined as a visceral or bodily (at times abject) reality, which reaches us in different ways at different times – not just a scientific fact, defined by the cessation of a heartbeat, but a personal, sensory, psychological and socio-ocultural experience.

A combined and condensed image of a foetus in a mother's womb and a grand-mother's death as experienced by a daughter and a granddaughter were presented mid-way through the matrix. This had a reparative force, contrasting with the many split off thoughts and images of a terrifying and mysterious death:

> I drew the image of a, a foetus inside the mother's stomach, and I thought – or the uterus – and I thought about the kind of symbiotic togetherness of the start of life and the complete loneliness at the end of life [......] um, it makes me think of my, my grandmother, and I was actually there when she died, or had died, she was in the process of dying, and uh, the ambulance crew were trying to resuscitate her and then, when they didn't get anywhere she was put in the ambulance and they drove her to the hospital. And my mother and I followed the ambulance and, and saw her body in the hospital, it had been laid in a bed and it was very peaceful, and obviously she had only just died so there was sweat on her forehead, and I remember touching her forehead, and you know she had perspiration, and was so warm. It was a very beautiful and strange moment in my life.

Death is shown here not as something alien and set apart from the living, but as a con-nected bodily and psychological reality for the bereaved where the humanity of the grandmother, even in death, is present through the sweat on her brow. The warmth and the sweat suggest a human, physical presence after death and a hope that death is not always a definitive moment but a process of dying. The moment 'when the spirit leaves the body' is in reality difficult to define. This image challenges assumptions about the existential loneliness of death showing that when and how death occurs are trans-subjective and inter-relational questions.

The circular connection of birth and death in the above extract commences with a duality – symbiosis at birth, loneliness at death. Yet there is a tradition of watching over the dying, and we place great meaning in this presence, a watchful attendance, at the moment of death. In this sense, the living person is the holding environment for the dead or dying person – as the uterus holds the foetus – and the person who dies is expelled from the world alone. If the living does not attend to the dying the transition is lost, as no one is there to witness the passing away. But the situation also keeps the living in a process of separation from the dead relative or acquaintance. The circle in this image is established through a link between uterine existence and death, and the inter-generational relationship between mother, daughter and grandmother. Connection and closeness are established through a reference to symbiosis between mother and child in pregnancy that can be compared to the closeness between the living and the dying person. The beginning and end of life transcend the initial duality and become linked in circularity through the imagery, connecting death to new life and making it less cruel. In Kleinian terms it becomes possible to experience it from a depressive position, as both hopeful and sad; it gives way to a new life, but is also a closure in itself. In this image, as in images from the other matrices, there is loneliness when the generations are out of touch with each other but an experience of intergenerational connectedness makes old age appear meaningful.

Conclusion

In our use of the visual matrix, we were able to move beyond typical split discourses concerning ageing, as reproduced in the research literature and in conventional wisdom. At the outset we had supposed that these dualisms could be attributed to the anxiety-provoking nature of the transitions of ageing, not only for ageing individuals but for families and institutions looking after the elderly and for welfare states. The visual matrices provided settings where these anxieties could be contained, and in doing so lent support to the original assumption and to the use of this method by showing that the fears associated with ageing could be confronted and a depressive ambivalence attained.

The dualities we noted earlier did constantly emerge in the matrices: life/living and death/surrender; hope/despair; being alone/ being in relationship; impotence in the face of ageing/struggling to be in control; suffering/pleasure; anxiety-induced blankness/ability to think in the face of painful experience. Sooner or later, however, they were integrated into a holistic train of thought. We have used three extracts, which differed in the quality of the anxieties referred to in each, (for example, it is easier to generate pleasurable images of retirement than of dementia). Nevertheless certain ideas reappeared. Primary amongst these was the theme of generation as fruitfulness, with an emphasis on the succession of generations within a family; on human relationships that accompany and transcend loss and isolation; and on the circularity of birth, life and death, incorporating ideas of the everlasting life beyond individual death, in continuity, human community and the natural world.

Using Kleinian theory, we have understood the fears and anxieties associated with ageing that may limit and exclude from thought the complexity of hard-to-bear experience. In turn this tends to impoverish the discourses available to policy-making and good-enough care, confining them to less painful or split representations of ageing as idealised or denigrated and hard to integrate. By contrast through integration of both bad and good facets of ageing, the matrix could give rise to the creation of new meanings and new experiences and help to enrich culturally available discourses.

In the visual matrix sessions, these processes were enacted in microcosm so that free associative successions of images oscillated between reassuring and anxiety-provoking visualisations of the challenges of death and dying, dementia and retirement. In varying measure, the images realistically reflected the positive and negative in these transitions. Closely linked, we could see patterns of movement between 'I' and 'other', affording closeness to, or distance from, the threats and satisfactions associated with ageing. The snowflake seating pattern, along with the shared affect and image-based format de-emphasised a sense of ageing as confined to the personal and produced associative, interconnected images that were sociocultural in character; that is, they represented challenges of ageing that could be recognised, related to and actively used by everybody while describing no person in particular.

As a post-script we should add that we, as a research group, were much affected by the visual matrices. The images and emotional states they produced in us continued after the workshops in the form of dreams and feelings, and sometimes an urge to share with others our experiences of growth and love. We explain this by the fact that we experienced the hard-to-bear aspects of our own ageing, vulnerability and mortality in a containing setting where inevitable anxieties could be brought into thought. We had the added advantage of successive sessions of immersion in the data, in a containing research group, for the purposes of analysis and this helped to intensify and deepen the experience.

The transformations that the research experience wrought in our relationships to ageing were enhanced by the richness of the images that the matrices so creatively generated; images that afforded multiple layers of condensed meaning that felt like an inexhaustible bounty. This aesthetic dimension seemed indivisible from the epistemological and the ethical (the immediate effect of the research on ourselves and other participants, and eventually, through dissemination, on the wider world). We hope that, hemmed in as this topic is by the fears and threats surrounding the transitions of ageing, we have managed to fashion images and ideas that address hard-to-bear realities while integrating positive and negative aspects. We hope that this will contribute to richer, more realistic and useful discourses on ageing, better linked to compassionate practical care.

Acknowledgements

We wish to thank Professor Linda Lundgaard Andersen, Roskilde University, for participating in the early phases of the project and Professor Burkard Sievers, Bergische Universitat, Wuppertal, for sharing his knowledge on visual methods. The International Research Group for Psycho-Societal Analysis has been a collective and long-standing psychosocial thinking space and brought several of us together for the application. Finally we thank all participants who shared their images and ideas in the matrix sessions.

Funding

The workshop series *Exploring Life Transitions in Old Age through a Visual Matrix* (2014–15) was funded by The Joint Committee for Nordic Research Councils in the Humanities and Social Sciences (*NOS-HS*) [ES524583]. It included researchers from Norway, Denmark and the UK. A final self-funded workshop was held in the UK to deepen the analysis.

Notes

1. Froggett, Manley, and Roy (2015) offer a detailed account of the methodology, along with its theoretical underpinnings and analytic protocols. A methodological paper is forthcoming on its use in this particular context (Ramvi et al., in press).
2. Ugebrevet Mandag Morgen, https://www.mm.dk/vi-har-ikke-europas-hoejeste-pensionsalder-lige-nu/ (Accessed 24.01.2016).
3. Translation A. Liveng.
4. Langer (1942/1948) described this form of symbolisation as 'presentational' in contrast to the 'discursive' symbolisation of language.
5. Bion (1970) conception of the container (discussed below) is key to understanding the nature of the setting provided by a visual matrix.
6. A short video illustrating the snowflake and associative process is available on YouTube at https://vimeo.com/97731002.
7. The theoretical principles are largely rooted in the object relations tradition, drawing especially on Winnicott (1971) and Bion (1967, 1970).
8. In Norse mythology Yggdrasil is the name of a tall evergreen ash tree which reaches above the skies in height, spreading its branches out wide, holding together the nine worlds of the cosmos. Yggdrasil has three roots, which go deep into the earth, connecting the tree with three wells, as well as gods and giants. Dew drops from the tree drips down into the valleys. Below one of the tree's roots lies Nidhogg, a monstrous and dark power in the form of a dragon-like creature. Nidhogg sustains itself by 'sucking the corpses of the deceased' (*Völuspá* p. 55) (Translated by Birgitta H Gripsrud). Nidhogg gnaws at Yggdrasil's roots attempting to kill the tree, but every night the Norns (maidens representing past, present and future) pour healing water from the well over the roots' wounds so that it does not rot. These Norns also carve into the tree the lifespans and destinies of infants. Despite constant attacks and threats like hail storms from above and Nidhogg's incessant bites from below, Yggdrasil retains its life force, standing strong.

References

Aadland, A. K., Ramvi, E. (2016). "Døden snakker vi ikke om". Sykepleieres opplevelse av møtet med døden i hjemmesykepleien. *Omsorg: Nordisk tidsskrift for Palliativ Medisin, 33*, 49–55.

Andersen-Ranberg, K., Birk-Olsen, M., Kronborg Andersen, C., Christiansen, T., & Strid, A. (2007). *Pårørende til demente En spørgeskemaundersøgelse om deres helbred og behov* [Relatives to persons suffering from dementia. A questionnaire study of their health and needs]. Copenhagen: Socialministeriet.

Behuniak, S. M. (2011). The living dead? The construction of people with Alzheimer's disease as zombies. *Ageing and Society, 31*, 70–92.

Bion, W. R. (1967). *Second thoughts*. London: Karnac.

Bion, W. R. (1970). *Attention and interpretation*. London: Routledge.

Canadian Partnerships in Dementia Care Alliance. (2015). *Re-imagining dementia through the arts*. [online]. Retrieved February 2, 2016, from https://uwaterloo.ca/partnerships-in-dementia-care/re-imagining-dementia-through-arts/re-imagining-dementia-through-arts-0

Chodorow, N. J. (1999). *The power of feelings*. New Haven, CT: Yale University Press.

Corner, L., & Bond, J. (2004). Being at risk of dementia: Fears and anxieties of older adults. *Journal of Aging Studies, 18*, 143–155.

Dahl, H. M. (2011). Who can be against quality?. In M. Ceci, C. Björnsdóttir, & K. Purkis (Ed.), *Perspectives on care at home for older people* (pp. 139–157). London: Routledge Studies in Health and Social Welfare.

Dahl, H. M., & Rasmussen, B. (2012). Paradoxes of elderly care. In A. Kamp & H. Hvid (Eds.), *Elderlycare in transition: Management, meaning and identity in work - a Scandinavian perspective* (pp. 29–50). Frederiksberg: Copenhagen Business School Press.

Demensalliancen. (2015). *Visionspapir*. [online]. Retrieved February 4, 2016, from http://demensalliancen.dk/wpcontent/uploads/2015/04/Visionspapir-2_Demensalliancen_DOWNLOAD

Erikson, E. H., & Erikson, J. M. (1998). *The life cycle completed: Extended Version*. New York, NY: W. W. Norton.

Esping-Andersen, G., & Andersen, G. E. (1990). *The three worlds of welfare capitalism*. Cambridge: Polity Press.

Etwil, P., Sørensen, H. S., & Mackie, M. (2011). *Ældrestyrken kommer, temaartikel. Statistisk Tiårsoversigt*. [online]. Retrieved February 4, 2016, from https://www.google.dk/search?q=%C3%A6ldrestyrken+kommer&sourceid=ie7&rls=com.microsoft:da-DK:IESearchBox&i.e.=&oe=&gws_rd=cr&ei=Tc4pV4PEDOzX6QSui5HYBw

Evans, D., & Lee, E. (2014). Impact of dementia on marriage: a qualitative systematic review. *Dementia (London, England), 13*, 330–349.

Fristrup, T., & Munksgaard, M. E. (2009). Alderdommen er ikke, hvad den har været [Old age is not, what it used to be]. In S. Glasdam, B. Appel Esbensen, & K. Andersen-Ranberg (Eds.), *Gerontologi: Livet som ældre i det moderne samfund* (pp. 76–91). København K: Nyt Nordisk Forlag Arnold Busck.

Froggett, L., Manley, J., & Roy, A. N. (2015). The visual matrix method: Imagery and affect in a group-based research setting. *Forum Qualitative Sozialforschung / Forum: Qualitative Social Research [S.l.], 16*, 1–34. Retrieved April 21, 2016, from http://www.qualitative-research.net/inde

Goodwin, J., & O'Connor, H. (2012). Notions of fantasy and reality in the adjustment to retirement. *Ageing and Society, 34*, 569–589.

Grenier, A. (2012). *Transitions and the lifecourse: Challenging the constructions of 'growing Old'*. Bristol: Policy Press.

Hollway, W. (2015). *Knowing Mothers*. London: Palgrave Macmillan.

Hollway, W., & Jefferson, T. (2013). *Doing qualitative research differently: Free association, narrative and the interview method* (2nd ed.). London: Sage.

Hollway, W., & Volmerg, B. (2010). Interpretation group method in the Dubrovnik tradition. *International Research Group for Psycho-Societal Analysis*. [online]. Retrieved April 21, 2016, from https://www.researchgate.net/publication/277090401

Holstein, M. B., & Minkler, M. (2003). Self, society, and the "New Gerontology". *The Gerontologist, 43*, 787–796.

Völuspá – Volvens spådom: Et dikt om verdens skapelse og undergang. (2008). Translation from Norse to Norwegian by A. Holtsmark. Reykjavik: Gudrun Publishing.

Jacobsen, M. H. (2010). Dødens Sociologi – udfordringer for sociologi, selv og samfund [The sociology of death - a challenge to sociology, self and society]. In P. Tanggaard Andersen & H. Timm (Eds.), *Sundhedssociologi* (pp. 251–287). Copenhagen: Hans Reitzels Forlag.

Jørgensen, C. R. (2012). *Danmark på briksen 1* [Denmark on the couch]. Copenhagen: Hans Reitzel.

Kaasa, S. (2008). *Palliasjon Nordisk lærebok 2* [Palliative care - a Nordic textbook]. Oslo: Gyldendal Norsk Forlag.

Kamp, A., & Hvid, H. (2012). *Elderly care in transition – Management, meaning and identity at work.* Copenhagen: Copenhagen Business School Press.

Klein, M. (1975). *Envy and gratitude and other works 1946–1963.* London: Hogarth.

Langdon, S. A., Eagle, A., & Warner, J. (2007). Making sense of dementia in the social world: A qualitative study. *Social Science and Medicine, 64,* 989–1000.

Langer, S. K. (1942/1948). *Philosophy in a new key: A study in the symbolism of reason, rite, and art.* New York: NAL Mentor.

Liveng, A. (2016). Aktiv aldring – en sundhedsskabende eller usynliggørende diskurs [Active ageing - a health promoting or invisible making discoure]. In S. Lehn-Christiansen, A. Liveng, B. Dybbroe, M. Holen, N. Thualagant, I. C. Aamann, & B. Nordenhof (Eds.), *Ulighed i sundhed – Nye humanistiske og samfundsvidenskabelige perspektiver* (pp. 147–174). Frederiksberg C.: Frydenlund Academic.

Lloyd, L., White, K., & Sutton, E. (2010). Researching the end-of-life in old age: cultural, ethical and methodological issues. *Ageing and Society, 31,* 386–407.

Moffatt, S., & Heaven, B. (2016). "Planning for uncertainty": Narratives on retirement transition experiences. *Ageing and Society, 1,* 1–20.

Molzahn, A. E. (2007). Spirituality in later life: Effect on quality of life. *Journal of Gerontological Nursing, 33,* 32–39.

Österlind, J., Hansebo, G., Andersson, J., & Ternestedt, B.-M. (2011). A discourse of silence: Professional carers reasoning about death and dying in nursing homes. *Ageing and Society, 31,* 529–544.

Pleschberger, S. (2007). Dignity and the challenge of dying in nursing homes: the residents' view. *Age and Ageing, 36,* 197–202.

Prince, M., Wimo, A., Guerchet, M., Gemma-Claire, A., Yu-Tzu, W., & Prina, M. (2015). *World Alzheimer Report 2015: the global impact of dementia – An analysis of prevalence, incidence, cost and trends.* London: Alzheimer's Disease International (ADI). [online]. Retrieved January 26, 2017, from https://www.alz.co.uk/research/world-report-2015

Ramvi, E., Gripsrud, B. H., Liveng, A., Lading, Å., Froggett, L., Manley, J., & Hollway, W. (in press). The Visual Matrix method in a study of death and dying: Methodological reflections.

Winnicott, D. W. (1971). *Playing and reality.* London: Routledge.

Wrede, S. (2008). *Care work in crisis.* Lund: Studentlitteratur.

Yalom, I. D. (2008). *Staring at the sun.* San Francisco: Jossey-Bass.

In a further exploration of the visual matrix method, Clarke explores a different kind of unknown, that of the receding shores of memory and self in dementia. Just as Liveng et al use the visual matrix to understand the ineffable yet unknown fact of our eventual destiny in death and what this means to our existence in life, Clarke explores the unknown of what is left of the Self in the course of a process of dementia. This is the story of 'A' and how he is able to become a person with a story to tell that creates the potential for relationships beyond that of his identity as a victim of dementia. In this study, Clarke explores how a person with dementia is given the tools for self-expression that avoid an emphasis on discourse and language. His story is told through pictures, a recreation of his life on film. In this film, memories of the past become feelings of the present. And through a visual matrix with NHS staff whose professional lives are dedicated to the care of dementia sufferers, the visual 'language' of the matrix resonates with and plays and weaves into the story of 'A'. A new life is created from the fading embers of the old. The nursing assistants who inhabit the clinical health space of an acute National Health Service assessment and treatment unit for people with dementia are able to enter a new space created by the visual matrix where other stories are made possible and new perceptions and therefore relationships can be engendered. Clarke shows how an expression that has been lost through the failure of language can be rediscovered and celebrated through images. In the case of 'A', we encounter a palpable excitement and engagement with the process of creating the film with Clarke's help; in the case of the visual reflections of the staff in the matrix we feel the wonder and desire to re-engage with 'A'. This new perception revealed in images and affect is not, says Clarke, limited to a single person's story. Instead the staff are able to transfer this new knowledge to their work as a whole, because apart from the story of A as a person, what is being discovered is a new language for sharing that we all can use. There is s sense of joy and wonder at this discovery which also gives rise to what Clarke identifies as a 'quasi-therapeutic' effect on the staff, which brings her to suggest that the visual matrix may have a use in training for dementia care, beyond its use in this study as a research method.

Carrie Clarke

RE-IMAGINING DEMENTIA USING THE VISUAL MATRIX

This article discusses the impact of a 'life-story film' – co-created with a person with dementia – on NHS staff's perceptions of the person, and by implication, their wider perceptions of people living with dementia. The study used an innovative research method, the visual matrix, to encourage hidden images, feelings and ideas to emerge. A complex, multi-layered experience emerged through rich metaphorical language, encompassing both personal and broader sociocultural understanding of dementia. An unexpected outcome was the quasi-therapeutic effect of the visual matrix on staff. The study suggests that the visual matrix may have potential to be adapted as a training tool in dementia care and that the fluid, associative and non-linear qualities of the visual matrix may prove an effective method for gathering the views of people with dementia, whose authentic voices are under-represented and difficult to gather using traditional research methods.

Introduction

Much has been written over the past three decades on the need for a less medicalised, more person-centred approach to dementia care. Kitwood and Bredin (1992), Kitwood (1997), Zeisel (2009) and Cheston et al. (2015) have all written on the importance of getting to know the person with dementia within the context of their life; the significance of personal meaning, having a role, feeling valued and experiencing a sense of belonging. These are identified as factors that may contribute to a more embodied sense of self, increased emotional and psychological well-being and, as Cheston et al. (2015, pp. 417–8) suggest, may act as a buffer against the 'existential realities of their current life'. This study is thus situated within the context of person-centred care, and wider debates about the value of non-pharmacological approaches in dementia care.

The research was undertaken in an acute National Health Service (NHS) assessment and treatment unit for people with dementia. The study aims to explore the impact of a 'life-story film' – co-created by a person living with dementia (referred to as 'A') and a health professional – on nursing assistants' perceptions of 'A', and by implication, their wider perceptions of people with dementia. In an environment of daily exposure to high levels of distress, there is an almost tangible circulation of affect amongst staff and patients. The research explores some of the complex, 'beneath the surface' (Clarke & Hoggett 2009) affective responses and relational aspects of their role. The process brought up questions about staff members' own support needs, and whether this methodology might be translated and utilised as a training tool within person-centred dementia care.

The research uses a participatory research method, the visual matrix (see below for further explanation), 'a tool that uses the visual imagination ... to reveal hidden or unexpressed ideas, feelings and emotions in research subjects', (Manley & Roy 2016, p. 1). I also draw on reflexive material, including a dream, from a research journal kept during the research period; imagery from these sources resonated with metaphorical language in the visual matrix and contributed to meaning-making during data analysis.

Ethics approval and consent

The project was given ethical approval from the host academic institution (University of the West of England – UWE), and from the NHS Trust's Head of Research and Innovation. Research participants were provided with written and verbal information about the study; written consent was gained, and audio material and transcripts were securely stored. The 'life-story film' used as the stimulus for the visual matrix was edited to remove obvious identifying features. Written consent was obtained from 'A's' nearest relative to use the film for research purposes.

Sample selection

Participants recruited to the study were six nursing assistants, the researcher (a qualified health professional within the same team) and a student health professional. Participants consisted of six females and two males, of varying ages and periods of employment within the service.

Methodology: the 'visual matrix'

The visual matrix is 'a method designed ... to allow for associative thinking and the expression of unspoken affect in a research context' (Manley, Roy, & Froggett 2015, p. 4). Froggett, Manley, and Roy (2015) describe it as a method suited to researching shared experiences, and suggest:

> In the arts, healthcare and social care the visual matrix has the potential to bring an experiential dimension to studies of impact, while offering insight into the questions of how and why impact occurs (p. 26).

The stimulus to begin the process of visual thinking for the visual matrix was a 'life-story film', which included still images, narration and animation that 'A' and I co-created. Participants were then invited to share images, associations and feelings which arose in response to the stimulus and research question. During the visual matrix, participants sit in a configuration known as the 'snowflake' pattern. Chairs are situated to avoid direct alignment with others; this encourages expressions to be offered to the space, and may help avoid some of the 'interpersonal dynamics' that often occur in more conventional group-based qualitative research approaches (Froggett et al. 2015, p. 1).

Images, thoughts, ideas and associations accumulate and are experienced as belonging to the group, rather than individuals. The matrix thus serves as a container for circulating affect generated by conscious and unconscious processes, with the host/ researcher also performing a 'holding' function. Following a short break, participants gather to share what Froggett et al. (2015, p. 21) refer to as 'resonances and dissonances' from the matrix, and some early emergent themes and connections are identified. This is the first stage of the data analysis.

The visual matrix is transcribed; shortly thereafter two separate research panels – in this case consisting of a psychologist colleague and a specialist mental health nurse who delivers training in person-centred dementia care to care homes – then revisit the transcript, with the aim of reducing researcher bias and remaining 'experience-near' (Froggett et al. 2015 p. 17). This continues the process of drawing out emergent themes, paying attention to affective responses, 'provocations' (a Lorenzerian term referred to by Hollway & Froggett 2012, p. 5), in which 'beneath the surface' thoughts, feelings and associations may be attempting to find 'embodied expression' (ibid.).

In this study, an additional external perspective was provided through academic triangulation with five colleagues from UWE, to try to avoid what Hollway and Jefferson refer to as 'wild analysis' (Hollway & Jefferson 2013, p. 154). As in the research panels, the visual matrix transcript was revisited, and each participant was given exclusive time to convey affective responses and emergent meanings arising from the data, before a group discussion.

Setting the scene

On first meeting 'A', I was struck by his small stature. His level of distress was intense: he would clasp me tightly, imploring me to 'help him'. The transference and countertransference were powerful: he was a 'boy' who needed to be loved and cared for by his 'mother'.

'A' responded well to specialist care and treatment. He frequently recounted his experience of evacuation during the Second World War; this was clearly a significant story for him. The film became his way of exploring this expression of self through image and narrative. As Manley (2009) says

> Even a still image moves through time in our thinking minds. So, subjective knowledge has a constant role to play in the interchanges between perceiver and perceived (pp. 84–85).

These 'interchanges between perceiver and perceived' (ibid.) resonated strongly with me during the making of the film, and I responded intuitively by drawing a series of images representing 'A' as an eleven-year old boy. These became the subject of two short, co-created stop-motion animations, which were incorporated into the film. Reflecting

FIGURE 1 Still from film. ©Carrie Clarke

on the character illustrated here (Figure 1), I remain curious about his presence and role in this study. The image, with its children's comic book-like quality – completely unlike my usual drawing style – arrived fully formed. It is interesting to speculate on whether 'A's' instinctive need to revisit this specific childhood experience – at a time in his adult life when he desperately needed an emotional and psychological 'anchor' – acted on my own unconscious processes and created a transitional bridge to visual matrix participants. I believe that this embodied, emotional re-enactment of 'A's' story may have spoken directly to participants of his current need to be psychologically held.

The life-story film

The following is a summary of the film content:

> It is wartime, and an eleven-year old boy is evacuated from an industrial cityscape to a rural farm, leaving behind his parents and the only life he has known. He is allocated to a childless couple, 'who treat him as though he were their own'; he becomes fully immersed with the life of the rural community, and forms a strong attachment to the people and the horses who work the land. He remains for five years, reluctantly returning to his birth family at the end of the war as a young man of sixteen. On his return, he finds 'he doesn't know his parents, and they don't know him'. The film ends with brief reflections on the course of his life, before coming full circle back to his life on the farm.

Dream – context

The experience of the visual matrix often has a reverie-like quality, and it is interesting to speculate on whether this created the conditions for the vivid dream – which I will refer to as an aspect of the data analysis below – I experienced immediately after the visual matrix and its transcription. An entry in my research journal at the time notes, 'I feel like I've been inhabiting the visual matrix, and it's been inhabiting me'.

The visual matrix, as Manley and Roy (2016) state, 'has emerged from the practice of social dreaming' (p. 1), initially through the work of Gordon Lawrence in the 1980s. Social dreaming refers to a particular way of sharing dreams. The accumulation of dreams, images and associations are shared during a 'matrix', and are experienced as belonging to the group rather than individuals; it is through this process that new meanings and thoughts emerge (Manley 2014, p. 323). This often allows for the expression of previously unconscious or hidden thoughts and feelings within the group or social context. It may be that the experience of shared, accumulative expressions of images, associations and feelings with colleagues during the visual matrix contributed to the metaphorical expressions of teamwork embodied in the dream that follows.

The dream

The dream is transcribed in my journal as follows:

> I'm looking at a map through the lens of a camera, which is zooming in and out of focus. The scene is a country village, where the entire central road has been turned over to vegetable growing. I am greeted by a musician, whom I know as a volunteer at the hospital. Every member of the community participates in nurturing the crops; nothing goes to waste. The musician tells me of a machine that processes waste matter into dried pellets – kept in a wooden box – which are used as fuel; it strikes me that everything and everyone has a role or purpose. There is a second box which contains small insects; our task is to 'herd' them by stamping on the ground behind them, creating vibrations that drive them on. I'm told they don't always like this, and may give a nasty bite; when we reach our destination, I'm pleased to find that I'm okay.

Images and metaphors contained in the dream encouraged me to take an open and curious approach not only to data from the visual matrix, but also to wider meanings around the needs of both people with dementia and healthcare staff. The notion of a community working together to nurture and harvest the crops, for example, presents a powerful metaphor for the nature of work on the ward, where team work and a 'nurturing', compassionate approach towards patients and colleagues play an essential part. At harvest-time, everyone has a clear role and a sense of communal purpose. Whilst this is hard work, it brings satisfaction and reward, but essential and integral to this is a need to feel 'valued' for the part one plays. It is interesting to speculate whether participation in the visual matrix with colleagues may have amplified the significance of the harvest metaphor, leading to my dream and whether the metaphor's affective resonance was contained by and transmitted through the transcript data to the research panel.

As the researcher, the sense of 'riskiness' I felt around using the visual matrix (this was my first experience of using this research method, and I was uncertain how my colleagues would engage with the process) also gained symbolic expression in the insect scene of the dream, but I am relieved to have come through the experience and find, as in the dream, that 'I'm okay'. Could it be that the dream may also have served as a container for my own anxiety within the research context?

As I reflect on the dream, I am struck by a sense of ambivalence; the boundaries between the visual matrix, with its shared imagery and associations, my own dream world and the research process appear permeable, so that the dream becomes paradoxically both content and method, enabling new connections and insights. And viewed from another perspective, this sense of permeability, of undefined boundaries and fluid association across non-linear time, may give a glimpse of what it might mean to live with dementia. These fluid characteristics suggest that, as a research methodology, the visual matrix may be well suited to capturing the lived experience of people with dementia.

Non-linearity

The concept of the 'scenic rhizome' (Froggett et al. 2015, pp. 14–15), used to describe the fluid nature and transformative qualities of the visual matrix, reflects the associative nature of the visual matrix, which encourages both personal and social, conscious and unconscious processes. By its nature, rhizomatic growth occurs beneath the surface, spreading in all directions; it is, above all, non-linear. This has interesting implications for improving our understanding of the experience of dementia, for when linear thinking is unavailable or difficult to access (as in dementia) and time loses its sequential nature, then free association and other non-verbal forms of communication may create new ways of meaning-making.

Whilst the visual matrix is a research method and not therapy, it nevertheless draws on psychoanalytic thinking such as Hollway and Jefferson's (2013) discussion of the defended subject and researcher, projection and splitting in a research context and Menzies-Lyth's (1988) work on defences against anxiety in both nurses and institutions. The concept of a social unconscious (Weinberg 2007) and Hollway's (2013) notion of 'societal-collective processes' provide interesting commentary on 'circulating affect' within groups, which will be explored later in the paper. One unexpected but interesting finding from the study was how the visual matrix appeared to have a quasi-therapeutic effect on staff, an area that warrants further exploration.

Containing anxiety

Menzies-Lyth's (1988) collected works on containing anxiety in both nurses and institutions is particularly pertinent to this study. She writes 'By the nature of her profession the nurse is at considerable risk of being flooded by intense and unmanageable anxiety' (p. 50). Menzies-Lyth identifies that the healthcare environment generates a wide range of often conflicting emotions, such as 'compassion and love; guilt and anxiety; hatred and resentment...' (p. 43). The affective intensity is noted, including projected anxieties of both patients and relatives contained by the nurse. Menzies-Lyth (p. 51) suggests that a focus on task performance may be a form of psychic defence against anxiety; it 'splits' the nurse from the patient and thereby de-personalises the relationship. In this study, as a defensive 'split' occurs, the visual matrix acts as a container for overwhelmingly intense affect, discussed below.

On an organisational level, Menzies-Lyth observes similar defences; by 'disregarding the idiosyncratic social and psychological resources and needs of each unit' (1988, p. 53), a similar 'depersonalisation' takes place. Similarly, Obholzer and Roberts (1994, p. 12) writing on unconscious processes in healthcare environments, state:

> Like individuals, institutions develop defences against difficult emotions which are too threatening or too painful to acknowledge. These emotions may be a response to external threats ... They may also arise from the nature of the work and the particular client group.

Memory and time

Bergson's writing on the nature of memory and time provides interesting commentary on the fluid temporal and sociocultural connections between the person with dementia, the participants and researcher that were facilitated through the visual matrix. For Bergson (1912/2007, p. 91) 're-remembering' involves action and movement; each retelling differs and therefore becomes part of one's present. Bergson (1912/2007, p. 24) argues

> ...there is no perception which is not full of memories. With the immediate and present data of our senses we mingle a thousand details out of our past experience.

Participants and researcher each bring their own life experiences, which inevitably shape subsequent conscious and unconscious responses. Bergson continues,

> to perceive consists in condensing enormous periods of an infinitely diluted existence into a few more differentiated moments of an intenser life.... (p. 275).

I would suggest that this is what participants experienced through the visual matrix; five years of A's long life, described by one participant as 'probably the smallest part of his life really ... five years ... but maybe it's the biggest part as well'. The capacity of the visual matrix to contain such ambivalence and paradox was striking.

Findings: emergent themes

Loss

At every stage of the data analysis – the post-matrix discussion, the research panels and triangulation with academic colleagues from UWE – 'loss' emerges as a central affect, although its prominence fluctuates. Speaking during the visual matrix of her associations to the theme of evacuation, one participant offers an image of a mother and son walking away from the viewer: 'a mum and her son holding hands, that stuck ... it's that bond, isn't it'? There are perhaps echoes here of my own experience of transference and countertransference discussed earlier.

For another, loss takes on other forms:

> ...although he had to go back to his parents, he wasn't just leaving the [evacuee] family, he was leaving the horse, you know ... we all love our animals. So it would've been hard for him to go back, like he felt he should've, but he didn't want to...

There appear to be strong (paradoxical) affective resonances and associations generated during the visual matrix, which accumulate in intensity through sharing. Yet another participant implies an existential dimension to the sense of loss, which poignantly resonates with what it might mean to live with dementia:

> when he went back to the city and he lost nature he might have lost a part of himself.

Just as in the dream image, so here do I imagine the camera lens zooming out to take in a wider perspective. During the post-matrix discussion, participants consider the situation of 'A' and others, some seventy years later, living with dementia and in a strange hospital environment. There is universal acknowledgement of what dementia might mean to both the individual and his family: loss of self, roles, meaning, relationship and sense of belonging. The sense of loss is exacerbated by a hospital admission, as the person with dementia is removed from familiar people and places, which may function as psychological anchors in an increasingly confusing world.

One member of the research panel notes that 'loss' is often associated in the language and imagery of the visual matrix with feelings of 'happiness'. However, she

> kept thinking, how is that [happiness] there? I just feel really sad about his whole experience. How can he talk about it with so much happiness? I find that really difficult.

Relationship

Closely connected to the theme of loss, the subject of relationship is also considered significant. 'A's' relationships – to Bill and his wife, the rural community, the horses and the land – appear to have been disrupted or broken, resulting in a sense of 'rootlessness' expressed during the visual matrix:

> He wasn't just leaving the family, he was leaving the horse, you know, the animals.

> You wonder as well, if that helped him choose the RAF? It took him out of the city and all over the world; that probably helped him, being in the open air and not enclosed.

> Like you say, joining the RAF, you couldn't get further away really, could you?

The imaginings around 'A's' career choice appear to continue the extended metaphorical ambiguity around evacuation and belonging, as participants move fluidly between personal and socio-historical associations.

Participants in the visual matrix recognise that 'A's' experiences on the farm gave him 'a purpose, collecting the eggs and working with the horses', with clear roles connecting him to the wider community. Associations are made in the post-matrix discussion to the nursing assistant role, where participants feel that the meaning and value they attach to their role can become obscured by external socio-political pressures such as service funding, which in turn leads to internal (ward-based) defended practice, such as increased task-orientation rather than 'quality time with patients'.

The sense of 'not belonging' experienced by 'A' on his return to his birth family brings to mind the experience of dementia, which often leads to social isolation and what Simpson and French (2001, p. 62) describe as being 'on the edges where known meets unknown in our shared experience'. It also brings to the surface uncomfortable feelings in relation to the nursing role on a dementia ward; a place of uncertainty, fragile identities and close proximity to death.

For one visual matrix participant, the experience of thinking about 'A' and others living with dementia stimulated a strong affective response, expressed through personal associations to the cultural realm. The relationship between a young man and horse in the film 'War Horse' symbolised her own close relationship with her son, with whom she had recently watched the film 'about fifteen times'.

For another visual matrix participant, images of horses in a rural landscape stimulated 'memories' of relationship to a grandmother never known; these were unbidden associations, full of affective resonance:

> My gran was the youngest child. She loved helping her dad with the horses; she would walk behind when he was ploughing. It was a tiny house, you know, with an open fire in the middle. But the horses – she loved them, just like the boy in the film, and it so reminded me of her.

These associations suggest that attunement to embodied, affective responses may enable staff to develop the quality and nature of relationships needed by patients on the ward, which may include the 'holding' function identified by Winnicott (1971, p. 111) as essential to emotional development. This notion resonates with a study by Cheston, Thorne, Whitby, and Peak (2007, p. 448) undertaken with residents with dementia in a care home, which identified a 'dearth of emotionally sustaining relationships available ... when their relatives were not present'.

Refugees and evacuation

During the visual matrix feelings of anxiety and fear, and the need for security in relation to the war and evacuation come to the fore:

> You don't know whether [your family] would still be alive when you got back. You don't know if there's going to be bombs dropped at any moment...

> ...he was able to feel safe; whilst some of the cities were being bombed, he felt safe and secure...

...He slept in the attic [in the farmhouse], but it wasn't cold up there, because there was the fire beneath his bedroom, and, um, I felt that sort of symbolised how warm and content he was there.

The word 'evacuation' is itself ambiguous, simultaneously meaning a movement from danger to safety, but also 'the action of depleting or emptying' (Onions 1973). This typifies the way in which the image-based thinking of the visual matrix enables expression of that which may be hard to define through words alone.

For members of both research panels, affective associations to the experience of child evacuation during the Second World War brought to mind topical images of refugees, which simultaneously conveyed affective associations to dementia:

...this mass movement of refugees, and well, people facing death and danger. And, I mean, that's the whole thing about dementia, isn't it, you know, it's terminal, isn't it?

For a member of the first research panel, the shared affect appears to accumulate in intensity around the notion of evacuation:

I can't help but relate it to dementia; that sense of being 'evacuated' from your life and from everyone around you, having no choice about it, and just losing that control ... It sounds like the whole evacuation process *is* dementia, that's what I just keep trying to make sense of ... I feel like this ... is happening to him again now.

The parallels with what it might mean to live with dementia are recognised with what can only be described as a collective, embodied 'jolt'; the experience of fear generated by uncertainty, by loss of connection to people and place, and a need for emotional, psychological and physical safety.

Here we can see the way in which the associative and affective qualities of the visual matrix are contained within the transcript, and when revisited by subsequent research panels, become embodied. By remaining close to the experience of the visual matrix, complex layers of meaning – that are felt as well as known – can emerge, bringing together past and present, the personal and the universal.

'Harvest-time' as an embodiment of relationship, role and belonging

Throughout the visual matrix and subsequent data analysis, the image of 'harvest' resonated strongly, representing notions of community, working together, having a role and feeling valued. In the visual matrix, this is described as

...feeling that he was able to do something to be part of that community. And to be part of that team that made things go right, you know, collecting the eggs and so on. And they were all doing their bit for the war effort, so maybe that's why his little role was so important.

During the visual matrix, post-matrix discussion, research panel and in the dream described earlier, 'harvest' becomes a metaphor for the ward team and nature of work on a ward for people with dementia. This is a 'bittersweet provocation'; participants recognise the staff team needs to 'work together for the greater good'. However, staff shortages may make this challenging, resulting in increased stress and often a sense of 'feeling unvalued' by others, or indeed by themselves.

For me, the imagery of my dream creates an affective connection to the notion of 'harvest' as a metaphorical unifying force expressed in the visual matrix. Harvest-time brings together the whole community, and is considered so crucial to its sustainable functioning, that the entire heart of the village (the 'main road') is given over to this nurturing activity. The dream appears to reflect an overwhelming but unspoken need for relationship, belonging and purpose in both the person with dementia and staff, a need echoed in the dream-like expression of one visual matrix participant,

> And I wonder if he ever wonders whether he would have been a different person, because those years he was on the farm has made him who he was later on … It makes you think, they managed with so little, yet they were so happy…

Language as both conscious and unconscious communication

During both research panels and academic triangulation that followed, several 'tonal shifts' were noted in the transcript, with one in particular experienced as a 'dissonance' or 'provocation'. The panel was struck by the way in which participants expressed a strong sense of 'loss' and 'sadness', but in almost every instance counter-balanced this with paradoxical expressions of 'happiness', suggesting an instinctive need to 'make things better'; a possible defence against anxiety.

The provocation occurs with a recognition of the depth and multiplicity of 'ruptures of dislocations' (Ingold 2007, p. 169) experienced by 'A', and that his hospital admission is yet another repetition of this pattern. There is identification with and of the sense of helplessness and 'loss of control over his life' experienced as a boy, as a young man and again in his experience of dementia, which is acutely distressing. As healthcare workers, there is an instinctive need to care, to make better; but the terrible truth of dementia is that there is no recovery. Acceptance of this truth is an acknowledgement of the fragility of our own identity and proximity to death. In the visual matrix, the pain of this becomes overwhelming and with this collective, unconscious recognition, a 'splitting' appears to occur, as the group adopts a paranoid-schizoid position, in which all that is 'bad' accumulates and is projected onto the 'city':

> …all that smoke you know.

> And of course his first job when he went back was in the cinema, in the dark with this one light shining down, quite dark and

> Very enclosed.

> Suffocating … Long pause.

67

An analysis of the language of the visual matrix shows a distinct 'split', summarised in Table 1:

TABLE 1 Splitting and projection embodied in the language of the visual matrix

Country ('Good')	City ('Bad')
Community, harvest	Faceless, row after row of houses, alone
Warmth, fire	Cold
Colour	Black and white, grey
At the heart of things	Suffocating
Sunshine, light	Dark, smoke, rain
Spacious	Enclosed, crowded, on top of one another
Freedom	Enclosed, nowhere to go, no choice
Feeling valued	Feeling unvalued
Belonging	Alienation

As these dichotomous descriptions gain momentum, more participants collude and the affect increases in intensity; even the weather assumes a different character in an urban setting:

Terraced houses can make you feel very on top of one another, can't they?

Definitely.

Row after row of houses...

And miserable ... and if it rains, it's miserable in the city.

This sense of obfuscation accumulates in the visual matrix and is echoed in this participant's perception of dementia:

...he had such a good life, and he learnt so much, and this illness is taking that away from him. You know, how someone who really enjoyed life ... is slowly fading away.

The research panel notes a change in 'register'; the language becomes depersonalised and generic, and 'A', whose presence until this point has been strongly felt, becomes obscured by the 'smoke' of the city, and we 'lose sight' of him.

On re-reading this point in the transcript, I became conscious of 'collusion' between participants, myself included, reflected in the imagery. In the following extract, the laughter indicates a momentary intrusion of rational reflection, which becomes submerged beneath the affective content:

It's quite strange, because even though I know there was a range of black and white and colour photos, in my mind the country ones are all in colour and the sun's shining *[laughs],* whereas in the city it seemed quite grey.

These shifts of focus bring to mind the dream-image of the 'camera' moving in and out of focus, which appears synchronous with levels of affective intensity. In descriptions of the countryside, the quality of 'light' brings sharp detail into focus, whilst sweeping panoramic shots reflect 'spaciousness' and 'freedom'. Conversely, the grainy, black and white shots of the city lack definition; the field of vision is small, 'closed in' like 'rows of terraced houses'. It is through this imagery-rich language that the circulating affect becomes embodied, and demands that its presence is felt.

Fluidity

The apparent permeability within and beyond the visual matrix, and between the transcript and my own associations and dreams, are suggestive of the concept of the scenic rhizome referred to earlier in the paper. I am conscious of the way in which there is at times a blurring of boundaries in my reporting of the different stages of the visual matrix and its analysis. This has led me to reflect on the complex interplay of my multiple roles and relationships during this research project. At the heart of it all is my therapeutic relationship with 'A'. This led to a new role, as co-creator of the film, which became the stimulus for the visual matrix, in which I was a participant alongside my healthcare colleagues, as well as researcher. It may be that my place in this intricate relational web – particularly as co-creator of the stimulus for the visual matrix – has reinforced for me the interconnectedness of the parts to the whole, making it hard at times to disentangle.

During the visual matrix, images of water came to my mind, and in recordings in my research journal watery imagery abounds. Ripples feature strongly; circles that are separate yet intrinsically connected by movement emanating from the centre. Recurrent images, words and feelings are experienced as reflections mirrored in water, with deeper meanings beneath the surface. There is a sense of temporal and spatial fluidity, as past and present 'melt … into one another' (Bergson 2001, p. 100). And confluence, where images, thoughts and associations from different sources converge, becoming a shared 'pool'. It is an immersive experience.

It is as if the qualities of 'reverie' experienced in the visual matrix permeate beyond its boundaries. As Crociani-Windland (2009) suggests, psycho-social researchers need an 'attention to fluid processes, affective responses, implicating both body and mind' (p. 68), which facilitates an understanding of the whole in relation to its parts.

Initially during the visual matrix, and subsequently during the research panels, I experienced a sense of elasticity – of both tension and fluid movement – between paradoxical elements, which altered in relation to affective intensity. This was an embodied sensation, a 'pushing-pulling' movement from my stomach and chest. Elasticity simultaneously enables closeness and distance, and movement between these two states of tautness and relaxation. This association/feeling may have been stimulated by the way participants were repeatedly drawn back to the paradoxical nature of 'A's' experiences, and the way in which nurses' defended positions create a tension between wanting to remain near, but simultaneously distant from patients. This may represent a transition to the 'depressive' position in the researcher and visual matrix participants, suggesting an acceptance of the coexistence of good and bad in the whole.

A research journal entry immediately following the visual matrix records an association to an umbilical cord; interesting in relation to my earlier reflections on transference and countertransference. Triangulation with academic colleagues added depth to possible meanings; for one, it brought to mind 'spiritual midwifery', in which the nurse eases the passage between life and death, suggestive of Simpson and French's 'liminal space' 'the edge between the known earthly realm and the unknown spiritual realm (2001, p. 58). This prompts a question: 'What if we consider the person living with dementia as inhabiting a liminal space – a space between life and death'? Seen from this perspective, the needs of those living with dementia, and the skills required of staff, assume a very different hue.

Specific value of the visual matrix as a research method

Informal conversations with participants on their experience of the visual matrix continued during ensuing weeks. Fears of having 'nothing to say' were confounded, as participants found 'it all just kept coming from somewhere'. Similarly, concerns over 'saying the wrong thing' or being 'judged' were unfounded.

Participants were struck by the 'non-judgemental, respectful and supportive' nature of the experience, which appeared to reinforce a sense of belonging, of being part of a team; they expressed that they would 'like to do more'. This suggests further potential therapeutic benefits, which have not yet been explored. Through the visual matrix process, staff identified an overwhelming need for a regular, shared space in which to explore intense affect generated by the nature of their work.

The visual matrix facilitated participants to 'step into the person's shoes' and 'fill the gaps', affording a unique quality of attention towards 'A'. It allowed multiple perspectives and layers of meaning to coexist, providing rich data with a strong affective element, which was expressed both consciously and unconsciously. There was movement between one person's experience, shared in the retelling, to a weaving together (Froggett et al. 2015, pp. 5 and 9) of multiple personal and sociocultural associations.

The use of research journal material, whilst subjective, nevertheless resonated strongly with – and added depth to – the complex, layered meanings that emerged from the visual matrix. These were primarily experienced as 'affective ripples' emanating from the centre – the person living with dementia.

Whilst the data that emerged from the visual matrix was rich in its emotional colouring, it contained less in the way of images and associations than had been expected. My sense is that the powerful narrative voice in the life-story film led to an unspoken tension between the visual and the spoken, which may have made visual thinking less accessible. Further conflict may also have been generated by the paradox of using a film – by its nature linear – in the context of the non-linear visual matrix. To counterbalance this, future research using film could consider the example of Manley and Roy (2016, p. 3), who have used drawing to 'bridge the gap' between the images and post-matrix reflective dialogue.

Conclusion

The visual matrix created the opportunity for me, as researcher, to experience a shared journey with staff 'towards an understanding of hidden, complex and difficult to express emotions related to their work' (Manley & Roy 2016, p. 3). Participants' responses to the life-story film, given expression through the visual matrix, enabled access to and expression of often embodied affect that might otherwise have remained 'beneath the surface'. This suggests that the visual matrix may unintentionally have had a quasi-therapeutic effect on staff, an area that would benefit from further exploration.

Staff valued the way in which the experience allowed them to 'go deeper', leaving them 'wanting to know more'. They recognised that the context of a person's life, of what holds significant meaning, resonates with and informs the present, thus enabling a better understanding of expressions of distress, and how current needs might be met. This indicates a shift away from defensive practice towards a more relational approach to care, and suggests that there may be potential for adapting the visual matrix approach beyond the research field for use as a training tool within person-centred dementia care.

The visual matrix, which encourages image and affect rich associations across non-linear time, appears to have some commonality with the experiences of people living with dementia, a population whose authentic voice is rarely heard and is difficult to gather using traditional research methods. As a research method, the visual matrix is recommended as a tool for gathering evidence for effective psycho-social interventions in the field of dementia; it will be fascinating to see where this leads.

Acknowledgements

MSc funded by Health Education South West. With many thanks to 'A' for sharing his story, and his family for permission to use the film, to colleagues for their willingness to take a step into the unknown, to Lita Crociani-Windland for her support and inspiration, and to Julian Manley for his expert guidance.

References

Bergson, H. (1919/2001). *Time and Free Will: An Essay on the Immediate Data of Consciousness*. New York: Dover.

Bergson, H. (1912/2007). *Matter and memory*. New York, NY: Cosimo.

Cheston, R., Thorne, K., Whitby, P., & Peak, J. (2007). Simulated presence therapy, attachment and separation amongst people with dementia. *Dementia, 6*, 442–449. Retrieved February 28, 2016.

Cheston, C., Christopher, G., & Ismail, S. (2015). Dementia as an existential threat: the importance of self-esteem, social connectedness and meaning in life. *Science Progress, 98*, 416–419.

Clarke, S., & Hoggett, P. (Eds.). (2009). *Researching beneath the surface. Psycho-social research methods in practice*. London: Karnac.

Crociani-Windland, L. (2009). How to live and learn. In S. Clarke & P. Hoggett (Eds.), *Researching beneath the surface: Psycho-social research methods in practice* (Chapter 3, p. 68). London: Karnac.

Froggett, L., Manley, J., & Roy, A. (2015). The visual matrix method: Imagery and affect in a group-based research setting. *Forum Qualitative Sozialforschung / Forum: Qualitative Social Research, 16*, Art.6. Retrieved February 20, 2016.

Hollway, W. (2013). Locating unconscious, 'Societal-collective' processes in psycho-social research. *Organisational and Social Dynamics, 13*, 22–40. Retrieved March 16, 2016.

Hollway, W., & Froggett, L. (2012). Researching in-between subjective experience and reality. *Forum Qualitative Sozialforschung / Forum: Qualitative Social Research, 13*, Art. 13. Retrieved 20 February 2016.

Hollway, W., & Jefferson, T. (2013). *Doing qualitative research differently: A psychosocial approach* (2nd ed.). London: Sage.

Ingold, T. (2007). *Lines – A brief history*. New York, NY: Routledge.

Kitwood, T. (1997). The experience of dementia. *Aging and Mental Health, 1*, 13–22. Retrieved March 28, 2016.

Kitwood, T., & Bredin, K. (1992). Towards a theory of dementia care: Personhood and well-being. *Aging and Society, 12*, 269–287. Retrieved March 28, 2016.

Manley, J. (2009). When words are not enough. In S. Clarke, P. Hoggett (Eds.), *Researching beneath the surface: Psycho-social research methods in practice* (Chap. 4, pp. 84–85). London: Karnac.

Manley, J. (2014). Gordon Lawrence's Social Dreaming Matrix: Background, Origins, History, and Developments. *Organisational and Social Dynamics, 14*(2), 322–341. Retrieved December 22, 2016.

Manley, J., & Roy, A. (2016). The visual matrix: A psycho-social method for discovering unspoken complexities in social care practice. *Psychoanalysis, Culture and Society, 10*, 1–22. Retrieved December 22, 2016.

Manley, J., Roy, A., & Froggett, L. (2015). *Researching recovery from drug and alcohol addiction with visual methods*, In Hardwick, L., Smith, R. & Worsley, A. Innovation in Social Work Research, London: Jessica Kingsley.

Menzies-Lyth, E. (1988). *Containing anxiety in institutions – selected essays* (Vol. 1). London: FAB.

Obholzer, A., & Roberts, V. (Eds.). (1994). *The unconscious at work: Individual and organizational stress in the human services: By the members of the Tavistock Clinic Consulting to Institutions workshops*. London: Routledge.

Onions, C. (Ed.). (1973). *The shorter Oxford English dictionary on historical principles* (3rd ed.). Oxford: Clarendon Press.

Simpson, P., & French, R. (2001). Learning at the edges between knowing and not-knowing: Translating Bion. *Organisational and Social Dynamics, 1*, 54–77.

Weinberg, H. (2007). So what is this social unconscious anyway? *Group Analysis, 40*, 307–322. Retrieved March 28, 2016.

Winnicott, D. (1971). *Playing and reality*. London: Tavistock.

Zeisel, J. (2009). *I'm Still Here: A New Philosophy of Alzheimer's Care*. New York, NY: Avery (Penguin).

Clarke's use of a biographical film to stimulate a visual matrix can be compared and contrasted with Roy and Manley's use of movement to do the same. In both cases, the stimulus is wordless and the emphasis is on the affect that is elicited through something other than discourse. In Clarke's paper, the hidden memory of a dementia sufferer is brought out in a flow of poignant childhood memory which the visual matrix brings to the present. In Roy and Manley's paper there is a sense of embodied memory in physical motion, space and in relation to others. In both, verbal expression is deliberately superseded by forms of sensuous knowledge that more closely resemble Langer's description of the 'presentational' as opposed to the 'discursive'. 'Our sense-organs make their habitual, unconscious abstractions, in the interest of this "reifying" function that underlies ordinary recognition of objects...(Langer 1948, p.75). This is why, according to Roy and Manley, validity of the word 'journey' as a recognisable metaphor for recovery from substance misuse should be questioned through an analysis of what is allegorical and nomadic about recovery. Maybe recovery is not a 'journey'. Instead of a discursive representation of a recognisable 'journey', Roy and Manley suggest a more abstract and complex way of understanding recovery. The 'sense-organs' of the body in movement gain expression through the use of a language in the visual matrix which is 'presentational' despite its use of words. Roy and Manley demonstrate how the visual matrix uses words only to depict pictures and corresponding affect. In this paper, the visual matrix brings out a sense of the nomadic in recovery: movement without an explicit direction or destination but nevertheless not aimless. The aim behind this sensuous freedom of movement - both physical (external; the dance) and within (internal; the visual matrix) — can teach us to re-assess the value of attempts at foresight in social work, social care and health practice and to question the use of excessive target setting and outcome-based evaluations. The work undertaken by people in recovery from substance misuse with Fallen Angels Dance Theatre can, therefore, be understood as acts of relating, deeply bonding acts of intersubjectivity, 'bonds of love' (Benjamin 1988)... The beneficial effects of such work towards recovery were felt and experienced as authentic and joyous by the dancers. Such effects may be difficult to measure, but, as Roy and Manley show, they are cherished, existential and real enough to those people in recovery whose worlds are touched.

Alastair Roy and Julian Manley

RECOVERY AND MOVEMENT: ALLEGORY AND 'JOURNEY' AS A MEANS OF EXPLORING RECOVERY FROM SUBSTANCE MISUSE

The paper explores the quality of the affective and embodied experiences of a group of people in recovery from substance misuse as part of their involvement with dance and movement workshops provided by the Fallen Angels Dance Theatre. In the research we used the visual matrix method alongside individual- and group-based movement sessions so as to explore associations and affect emerging from the visual matrix. We question the frequently used metaphor of the 'journey' in recovery and suggest 'allegory' to be more apt. The linearity implied in journey contrasts with movements — both inner and outer — that are 'nomadic', 'wayfaring' and 'rhizomatic', focussed on affect and experience rather than targets and outcomes. We conclude that people working in the field of recovery and other areas of social work may wish to reconsider the value of embodiment in movement, relationship and affect when working with the experience of vulnerable people.

'Journeys', directions and destinations

This paper is concerned with the work of Fallen Angels Dance Theatre (FADT)[1], which exists 'to support those in recovery from addiction, to transform their lives, and to share recovery journeys with the wider public, through dance, performance and creativity'. In this paper, we wish to question the common use of the word 'journey' to describe a person's recovery from substance misuse. 'Journey' implies direction and destination, along with an implication of judgements about the right or wrong paths a person may follow in her 'journey' of recovery from substance misuse. We suggest that the idea of 'journey' is unhelpful as a description of what happens in the work of FADT, and that it may also be inappropriate as a general metaphor for recovery. Instead of 'journey', we will be suggesting 'allegory' as a description of the process of recovery, especially as a description of the experience of working with FADT. For FADT, dance and movement seek to raise the awareness of experience among those it works with. This experience of movement of the body is not a journey, since it leads to no place. In the work of FADT, movement is way of exploring experience in the world, where the purpose of movement is not directed towards reaching a certain destination or terminus, but used to bring what happens along the way into memory and 'conscious awareness' (Ingold, 2011, pp. 152 and 126–127).

We worked over two sessions with a group of people in recovery who were regularly attending workshops run by FADT in Liverpool, UK. We used the visual matrix method, which has been employed before in the context of recovery (Manley and Roy 2017; Manley, Roy, & Froggett 2015) and in other contexts (Froggett, Manley, & Roy 2015; and see Liveng et al. and Clarke in this edition) as a way of bringing visualisation and association rather than discourse to the fore in group-based reflection. In doing so, a space was created where the participants could express their embodied, affective experiences of recovery through visualisation and dance. This was a space of internal movement, internal thoughts and emotions, the 'movement inside' that could open out the possibility of relation and connection to the 'movement outside' (Manley 2013) of the dance itself.

Although the paper focuses on recovery from substance misuse, the issues are of relevance to a broad range of health and social work practice experiences, where the language of journey – with its implicit teleology of progress – is common. The use of the journey metaphor applied to people experiencing situations of extreme vulnerability might represent a form of 'cruel optimism' (Berlant 2011; Roy 2017), encouraging or inadvertently coercing people towards pursuing unrealistic aspirations, with those who fail to achieve them becoming targets of systemic disapproval and anxious self scrutiny (Espeland & Stevens 2008). We argue instead that, to work with the reality of the fragments or ruins of people's lives through the allegorical might manifest as a form of caring and hopeful pessimism, which reaches towards a potential for self awareness and personal development.

'Movement outside', dance and wayfaring

Dance contrasts to the movement implied in 'journey'. We will be asking in this paper to what extent the experience of the body in movement is in itself and by itself an experience of recovery. In doing so, we will also question the implications of the word 'recovery', if by this is implied a destination to be arrived at. Instead of the idea of 'recovery' as journeying towards a destination, we will be reflecting upon the idea that it involves a form of 'wayfaring' (Ingold 2007, pp. 75–84) in which someone in recovery 'negotiates or improvises a passage' as she goes along. This is what Deleuze called 'nomadology', later converted into 'nomadic theory' by Braidotti (2011). Nomadic theory conceives of thinking as embodied and embedded in the experience of self; it conceives of self as relational and non-unitary; it speaks to a turn of thought with its roots in post-modern continental philosophy towards affect and experience (Braidotti 2011, pp. 2–8). It also connects to the Deleuzian concept of the 'rhizome', that we use alongside the allegory to move away from the linear tendency behind the concept of journey. The rhizome describes the creation of paths without direction – the paths of the nomad – where important moments are those that come close to creativity through chance encounters and spontaneous events (Deleuze & Guattari 1988, pp. 21-15). The point for Ingold, referring to Deleuze, is that

'Life is open-ended: its impulse is not to reach a terminus but to keep on going. The spider spinning his web or the musician launching into a melody 'hazards an improvisation'. But to improvise, Deleuze continues, is to join with the World or meld with it. One ventures from home on the thread of a tune' (Ingold 2011, pp. 83–84).

'Movement inside' and interrelationality

Although actual physical dance is the essence of the recovery work of FADT, we mean more than this by 'movement'. In Braidotti's nomadic theory (2011) the concept of movement is used to suggest a quality of thought that goes beyond the Cartesian brain. According to nomadic theory, to understand movement as a means of thinking, we have to consider both the 'embodiment of the mind and the embrainment of the body (Marks 1998)' (Braidotti 2011, p. 2). Instead of focussing on each individual mind, experiential knowledge is gained though 'the relational motion of approaching multiple others' (Braidotti 2011, p. 2).

Where 'inhabitants meet, trails are entwined, as the life of each becomes bound up with the other. Every intertwining is a knot, and the more that lifelines are entwined, the greater the density of the knot' (Ingold 2011, p. 148). In this way human existence is not place-bound but place binding (Tilley 2004, p. 25). Creativity and vitality emerge from the wanderings of the 'nomad' over 'smooth spaces' (meaning spaces where movements are free and without direction), and where spontaneous chance encounters produce knots or 'intensities of affect' (Deleuze & Guattari 1988, pp. 474–500). It is in encounters such as these that the work of FADT – where recovery becomes a movement in relation to others – creates new perspectives and opportunities for creative changes to occur.

In our research we were asking if this relationality and encounter with 'multiple others' in the dance work of FADT was effective in supporting recovery. Through the sharing of mental images and affect in the context of a visual matrices, we were able to compare the internal movement of images and affect that weaved in and out of the mental space of the matrix, with the movement sessions. In doing so, we became conscious of the importance of the 'nomadic' process of the visual matrix and 'the dynamic nature of thinking and the need to reinstate movement at the heart of thought by actualising an non-unitary vision of the thinking subject' (Braidotti 2011, p. 7).

Allegory, images and emergent meaning

Through the use of the visual matrix method and the opportunity it gives participants to reflect upon experience through a dynamic encounter of images and affect among themselves, we are able to substitute the representational and cognitively conceived symbolism of 'journey' with the nuanced, incomplete and provisional visual fragments implied in 'allegory'. This difference is made clear in an extract from Walter Benjamin's

The Origin of Tragic German Drama, which tells us that allegory 'corresponds to a perception of the world in ruins, and is therefore the art of the fragment, and the opposite of the symbol, which presupposes the value of 'Nature' preserving unchanging, complete, identities and values' (quoted in Tambling 2010, p. 110). In allegory, importance is given to the experiences of unplanned discoveries and encounters rather than preordained steps towards a final destination. This is revealed to us at the start of one of the most famous allegories in literature, Dante's *Inferno*: 'In the middle of the journey of our life I came to myself in a dark wood where the straight way was lost', (quoted in Tambling 2010, p. 2). We will be looking at how the images that emerged from the visual matrix were used by the dance group as an allegory for their lives in the context of recovery, embodiment and movement. We will consider the validity of conceptualising the experience of substance misuse as one of movement and allegory and how the use of movement and dance in the practice of FADT can lead to wellbeing and a reassessment of the meaning of living a life in recovery. Finally, we seek to understand the special nature of dance and movement with people in recovery and how movement and dance contribute to allegorical aspects of recovery that begin with the complex image of the 'Fallen Angel', the tragi-daemonic figure of recovery in FADT.

The movement to recovery in the treatment sector

Our research was undertaken against a background of a sector that has moved from broad to narrow definitions of 'recovery' and where the practice of FADT might be seen as an interesting anomaly rather than in any way mainstream. In the UK since about 2005 there has been a steady move towards a recovery orientation in policy and practice. In early discussions – led by UK Drug Policy Commission in (2008) – about the ways in which a recovery orientation might inform treatment approaches and models of care, there was a desire to reflect the highly personal and idiosyncratic nature of addiction. This seemed to reflect a desire among many leaders in the sector to resist the possibility that a very generalising definition of recovery might be imposed by government as part of a new policy direction. By 2010 recovery had become a central strand of a new government policy and there was a stated emphasis on increasing the number of people achieving 'full recovery' (Monaghan & Wincup 2013), reflecting a governmental desire for recovery to become a specifiable destination (Roy & Buchanan 2015).

By 2016, a set of quantifiable measures of recovery had been produced (Neale et al. 2016) and subsequently a Substance Use Recovery Evaluator tool[2], which the authors suggested now made it possible to 'measure' the concept of recovery in an 'objective' and 'meaningful way'. In the development of measures and tools – albeit ones co-developed with service users – we see a desire to smooth over idiosyncratic difference and to fix meaning through quantification, in which recovery becomes something that can be measured – whether by the self or others – in an objective manner (Espeland & Stevens 2008). Although the idea of a quantifiable set of measures by which one can self-monitor recovery progress might be alluring to some who struggle with substance misuse, appearing to provide something concrete and secure, the shadow side of this might be failure, shame and humiliation in which 'The "outliers", "underachievers", and "under-performers" produced by performance measures become targets of ... disapproval and anxious self-scrutiny' (Espeland & Stevens 2008, p. 409).

In traditional 12 step programmes the 'journey' consists of a series of definable steps which are accompanied by a sense of a spiritual journey towards some form of redemption, akin to enlightenment. Although theoretically this is a journey which can have no endpoint or final destination – because in the Fellowships one is always a self-confessed addict – it is one measured in time travelled, in the public voicing of days since last use. It could also be argued that the 'journey' does in fact end in abstinence with a constant fear of 'falling' again. In 1961 Carl Jung wrote a letter to AA's co-founder in which he set out two main ways in which people with serious alcohol addiction might recover. One was through 'real religious insight', the other was through 'the protective wall of human community' which included 'personal and honest contact with friends' (AA, 1963 cited in Kelly, Hoeppner, Stout, & Pagano 2012, p. 296). Kelly et al (2012) suggest that

> although AA has more earnestly expressed the former as being the principal pathway to recovery ... perhaps inadvertently, stemming from its social orientation and structure, it has tapped also into the curative facets of the latter – protective and positive social influence (p. 8).

This helps frame the issues affecting people with substance misuse problems around human relationships rather than belief systems, steps or targets (Roy & Buchanan 2015).

Trauma, knowing and recovery

Taking into account the importance of relationships and embodied experience to recovery, we argue that a bio-psycho-social view of addiction seems relevant in engaging with a project such as FADT, which emphasises the long-term benefits of immersion in a community of fellow addicts. A great deal of research has confirmed a link between childhood experience of trauma and subsequent addiction. The attraction of drugs – initially at least – can lie in the ways in which they fix problematic feeling states in individuals, providing a sort of protective function which can create a powerful motive for continued use. This emphasises the idea that abstinence by itself might be insufficient in addressing substance misuse problems, because it addresses the coping strategy rather than the issue which led to its emergence. This opens out the possibility that the 'restlessness, paranoia and hypersensitivity' which often accompany both addiction and the early phases of recovery might be 'a body's testimony to its past' (Gunaratnam 2015) and one that needs to be revealed through the expression of embodied knowledge through relationships in movement, which is the very essence of the work of FADT.

We are interested, therefore, in exploring the idea that to know the self in addiction and recovery may well be the stuff of experience rather than intellectual knowing. The discussions we had with dancers at FADT brought to life the ways in which people in addiction can feel separated from others in the world; and that bodily knowing – undertaken in relationship with others – might be important in pursuing a knowing-recovery and establishing a connection with the world. Ingold (2011) makes a distinction between the quality of knowing through experience and the accumulated knowledge of cognition, arguing:

> To be sure, the expert is more knowledgeable than the novice. What distinguishes them, however, is not a greater accumulation of mental content – as though with every increment of learning yet more representations were packed inside the head – but a greater sensitivity to cues in the environment and a greater capacity to respond to these cues with judgment and precision. The difference, if you will, is not one of how much you know but how well you know.

The work of FADT recognises that successful recovery is not predicated on the acquisition of 'built-up' knowledge ('mental content'), but is based on a form of corporeal and embodied understanding which is built in the environment and through movement (O'Neill 2014; Roy 2016). People in recovery don't apply knowledge learned elsewhere to their daily recovery practice, but come to know 'along the way' and 'by way of' their experience (Ingold & Kurtilla 2000, p. 191–192).

Methodology

Since the aim of our research was to investigate movement and allegory in collaboration with FADT, we avoided methods focused on narrative, as well as methods with an *a priori* structure, such as semi-structured interviews and/or focus group discussions. Instead, we chose an approach – the visual matrix – likely to open up spaces of reflection, affect and hypothesis. As researchers we took on the role of facilitators or hosts in the visual matrix. We made two research visits to the FADT dance spaces being used at the time. In each visit we hosted a visual matrix, eliciting images from the participant dancers and performers. There were about 12 participants, male and female, between the ages of 20–50, and they were accompanied by two researchers and one FADT staff member/choreographer. The participants and researchers sat on randomly distributed cushions on the studio floor, thereby avoiding direct eye contact with each other and encouraging instead a 'speaking to the space'. In the visual matrix, participants are able to express spontaneous images and feelings as they arise, free associate and make links and connections between the images, without ever interpreting meaning or entering into cognitive discussions. In this way the visual matrix accumulates a collage of affect-laden mental images that creates a shared affective sense instead of a discursive, cognitive knowledge.

Each of the two visual matrices was followed by a different movement exercise. In the first, each individual was asked to develop and perform for the group a short movement piece which related to themes from the matrix. In the second, the response consisted in a collective improvisation in which the whole group moved together in response to the visual matrix as well as in relation to one another. In each case, participant expressions in movement and dance emanated from the visual matrix, but in the second session they also emanated from other people's movements.

The visual matrices were audio recorded and transcribed, while the dance and movements sessions were video recorded. We worked in a series of panels to analyse the transcripts of the visual matrices and compared these to the videoed movement sessions.

Allegory, movement and affect in visual matrix 1

The following analysis comprises quotations from a selected part of the visual matrix transcript that emerged through analysis as being especially illuminating. The participant contributions are transcribed exactly as and when they arose. Sometimes they consist of one word only; at other times a series of images are expressed in a sentence or two. Each separate intervention is marked by a dash.

We begin with an image of ice in the form of icicles which develops into a series of image-affects that accumulate and multiply through association:

Icicles

support

Brings to mind an artist who makes sculptures out of ice. They are so beautiful but they start to melt, drip by drip, and eventually, by the end of the day, they have melted away. It's both beautiful and then sad when it's gone.

The icicles that seem to be the opposite of 'support', so essential to recovery, are transformed into 'sculptures of ice' by an artist. In this way the unsupportive icicle is made into something supportive of beauty, aspiration and creativity. The agency of humankind – the 'artist' – is what makes this possible, conveying a powerful sense of the potential for creativity and therefore change. In the recovery context, the change is from a sense of melting away to something made and recognised. In this way, there is hope in the ability of each of us to create. Nevertheless, the image-affect is in no way naïve or idealistic, since even this creation is subject to erosion commensurate with the passing of time. This leads to the next association:

I'm reminded of that hotel made of ice. They have to remake it every year, it's something that keeps rebuilding.

In this case the ice construction becomes a useful shelter. Many in recovery will understand shelter as being a precarious asset. The shelter in the image-affect is a temporary one, a hotel, and rather than accept its erosion as in the previous image, in this case it is remade every year, an action that speaks to the need for continued work and perseverance as well as a facing up to reality, both qualities necessary to recovery. This brings up an association to Tibetan Buddhist sand paintings:

Brings to mind sand art. The Tibetans or Buddhists creating mandalas in the sand and then at the end of the day they brush it up and go.

The image reaches back to the artist evoked at the beginning of the sequence of associations, building up in this way the rhizomatic sense of connections. In a sweep of creative imagination the 'ice artist' becomes the 'sand artist', within which the sense of movement creates a tension between sensations of wet/cold and dry/hot and associates the artistic creative practice with some form of spirituality suggested by Buddhism. This may help us understand the need for some spiritual core or form of belief system to help people in recovery, and indeed the Fellowships traditionally emphasise spiritual-ity through Christian belief. At the same time, the association moves sequentially, with the rebuilding of the ice hotel being linked to the need to rebuild the sand mandala, which has to be destroyed. The repetition of the need to persist and rebuild, but this time in tension of the two extremes of wet/cold, dry/hot, emphasises the importance of these qualities in recovery both through the repetition itself and the all-encompassing extremes within which rebuilding has to occur. The powerful affect evinced at his stage of the matrix encourages the FADT choreographer, in his role as guide and mentor, to make a direct and overt link to the struggle of people in recovery:

> That brings to my mind how the Ego builds up so quickly in recovery and how you have to smash it every day, so you are rebuilding on the go every day.

The next image combines the previous artist/spiritual/ice image-affects in an image of the small rocks in a Zen garden which have found their way into a man made creation of peace and serenity after being formed by a glacier. In the image of the Zen Garden, created for contemplations of the meaning of life, we have a further rhizomatic accumu-lation and synthesis of the images of water and sand, since the Zen Garden specifically imitates the ripples of water in shapes delineated in sand or gravel:

> A friend of mine has a garden and small rocks in it, like a Japanese Zen garden style. They are stones from a glacial shift.

The fact that the stones come from a 'glacial shift' reminds us of the ice of the previous images and adds to their sense by turning what was originally a dripping icicle into a source of grinding power that has the capability of moulding stones into beautiful rounded objects that can subsequently be used for a Zen Garden.

Following this contemplative 'movement inside' implied in the meditation of a Zen Garden, the next associations remind us of the great distance, the 'movement outside', that has to be covered – even if it is in a slow, grinding movement – for a stone to be hewn into a shape, from some mysterious place lost in the past to Birmingham!

> You don't know how far they have travelled. In the long journey, and how they have been rounded.

> They start somewhere and they snake along and they are all taken down to some-where else, could come to somewhere else, like Birmingham.

In this way the physical movement, which is unknown in distance and has moved according to the whim of natural forces rather than to a set purpose and direction, is linked up with the internal movement of meditation and self reflection, where thoughts are allowed to flow rather than conducted towards a specific problem. In both cases, we have an example of nomadic activity, which has specifically emerged from the think-ing and affective space of the visual matrix. In terms of recovery, there is an appeal to creativity and movement that provides creativity as a means of reaching a space where recovery is made more possible than in situations of cognitive decision-making, target setting and programme design. As we have suggested above, it is precisely this kind of relational and somehow abstract knowledge that seems to work in the Fellowships (Kelly et al. 2012).

Allegory, movement and affect in visual matrix 2

One of the striking features of the second visual matrix was the exploration of the importance of the endurance of love in the passing of time, which is explored in images of water and wood. Once again, the movement of water, and whether this movement is free or restricted, is key to this reflection. This emerges from the very beginning of the matrix, where an immediate contrast is made between free flow and channelled flow:

> Strong images of water, water running down rocks and though the city. Then an image of a bridge. Water running through and a concrete sluice.

The channelling of the water seems to occur after the image of a bridge marking a 'before-and-after', and a sense of a loss of freedom. The sense of channelling life is expressed in an image of people following cracks in the pavement which are contrasted to ripples in the water and the added suggestion that the lack of footprints and therefore a sense of direction in movement, may be due to the action of the waves, 'water coming in and out':

> No footprints.

> People walking in and out of each other, like busy ants in the cracks of the pavement.

> Don't step on the cracks.

> Watching ripples.

> Waves coming in and out.

The reference later in the visual matrix to the mother's tears which is associated to an earlier image of a frozen tear, links the image of moving water to a tear of happiness, which is always in danger of becoming stilled through freezing:

> I have an image of my mum crying a single tear, a tear of happiness, watching it run, flowing and trickling on all the lines of her face and dispersing.

Later in the matrix, the relative stillness of a tree trunk is contrasted to the passing of time for two people in love; yet the quality of this love somehow resists the movement of time:

> Reminds me of an image of a nineteenth Century painting, where two old lovers are standing next to a tree, but the tree has aged, as the lovers have, and they can

see their names etched on the trunk, so you can see the passing of time as the names have aged with the tree.

Reminds me of an image of a nineteenth Century painting, where two old lovers are standing next to a tree, but the tree has aged, as the lovers have, and they can see their names etched on the trunk, so you can see the passing of time as the names have aged with the tree.

Image of an older couple and the love is still there, strange. They look tired and worn out but they are still together.

The water and tree images are connected in rhizomatic fashion by an image that expresses the wearing away of wood by water, eventually distorting the former useful-ness of the object:

Desolate, water-aged rotten wood that served a purpose.

What is striking about the way these image-affects work – according to a nomadic, rhizomatic collage of interlinked associations – is the way the complexity of existential human concerns, such as love and time can be brought to light and made relevant to the lives of the participants in FADT. Through understanding the value and impor-tance of an enduring love in terms of support to the participants in the matrix, a space of autonomy and empowerment is created for those participating in the matrix. They themselves are reflecting upon and identifying their own values through self-reflection instead of being advised or told by a third party who may be knowledgeable but inevi-tably distant to the experience of the individual in recovery.

The allegory of movement

The two visual matrices developed combinations of image-affects that together gave expression to the complexity of people's experience in recovery. The nature of this expression as a series of loosely attached image-affects oscillates between what Derrida called 'constative' and 'performative' iterations, the former being a 'discovering or un-veiling' and the latter a 'producing, instituting, transforming' (Derrida 1991, p. 206). The image-affects of the matrix have produced an 'essential instability' (ibid. p. 207) that comes from the shifting complexities of the language focus that Derrida would have called 'deconstruction'. The visual matrix works in a way that is similar to Derrida's de-scription of fable or allegory in his essay 'Psyche: Inventions of the Other' (ibid.). What can at first be 'perfectly normal in its grammar, spontaneously deconstructs the oppo-sitional logic that relies on an untouchable distinction between the performative and the constative and so many other related distinctions' (ibid. p. 208). For example, the smoothing of the rock into pebbles by glacial action that are then deposited in 'Birming-ham' is not so much a story of glacial erosion as an expression of the affect contained in the quasi-symbolisation of beauty, perseverance and change against all odds achieved through gradual transformation (rough rock to smooth pebble); and then, through as-sociation, these pebbles, gravel and sand are made into a Zen Garden, a symbol of inner peace and quiet meditation. The shared nature of the hope and yearning desire implied in this transformation is, in normal circumstances, emotionally and conceptually difficult to express, especially for people in the midst of the anxieties and emotional upheavals that are part and parcel of the experience of recovery.

Working with the visual matrix and dance movement created a shared space for the exploration and expression of these allegories in the first matrix. Similarly, existential concepts of time and love, which are perhaps not uppermost in standard discussions between people in recovery and staff from supporting agencies, emerged as important themes in the second visual matrix.

C.S Lewis' seminal work *The Allegory of Love*, (1936), describes the use of allegory as an exploration of the complexities of love. Lewis pointed out how mediaeval texts always operated on two levels, a superficial narrative or story level accompanied by a sub-text of rich, loosely connected images and symbols that were representative of emotional realities which were not necessarily part of the sequential actions of the narrative. These loosely connected allegorical images are dependent for their meaning to emerge on a free-flowing movement between the related parts. In our research, we saw how this kind of movement inside the 'body' of the space of the visual matrix was replicated in the movement and dance work of FADT. In one interesting contrast, we noted how the movement of the dance interpretations from the dancers was different in the two sessions we participated in. The first, which was framed around individual performance, led to story-like performances, which captured a singular theme – for example a metamorphosis. The second, framed around an improvised, simultaneous group exploration, began with loosely connected individual movements, which later became intensified as they were brought into relation and interaction with those of others in the group. In this way, the second movement session somehow mirrored the rhizomatic interconnectivities of the visual matrix by extending the sense of the image-affects into bodily movement, allowing for a continuation – in movement – of the complex and overlapping exploration of the matrix. This sense of rhizomatic interconnectivity and how this emerges from associations rather than sequential narrative was noted by one of the participants in the second session:

> Associations, my brain is a big joined up spaghetti. (Participant, FADT)

In both the movement improvisation exercises and the inner 'movement' of the affect in the matrix the relational and sharing process takes sensation away from being a purely subjective, personal experience to another understanding of 'body', the body of inter-connected and related forces:

> Sensation in the body does not belong to the subject. Sensation or feeling belongs rather to a sensibility of forces that is expressed in the genesis and emergence of their relations with one another ... affect and sensation are thus discerned in the body, in each body, but also in the context of other, emerging bodies... (Rothfield 2011, p. 211).

The idea of such a shared affective space as that which is experienced in dance improvisation and the sharing of image-affects in a visual matrix, is a powerful way of understanding the value of bonding and sharing among peers. Given the relationship we identify between trauma and addiction and the tendency to use substances to fix feeling states such as personal anxiety, it is easy to see why people pursuing recovery might benefit from the movement activities of FADT. Recovery, our research suggests, has more to do with companionship, relationships, bonding, creating safe spaces and spirituality rather than a dogged pursuit of quantifiable targets and goals. Our research indicates that it is the embodied joy of inner and outer movement in relation to the self and others that makes the FADT programme so attractive and beneficial to participants. We can see this effect in the following comment from another participant who described the experience of combining the image-affects of the visual matrix with movement as being at once creative, intuitive and spiritual:

> Loved it – Felt in touch with pure creativity, intuition. Felt like a spiritual exercise (Participant, FADT).

Spirituality, intuition, 'pure creativity' and a sense of absolute joy are not necessarily commonly valued features in substance misuse programmes, which instead might be more concerned with quantifiable and objective measures of things such as substance misuse, self-care, relationships and outlook on life. Approaches based on measurement are all associated with the journey metaphor we began this article with. This is an attitude with its roots in Cartesian reason and logic, which favours the simplification and reduction of emotional material into sequential narratives of cause and effect. As we see in our work, these cannot do justice to the complexities of the experience of recovery. Instead, we have drawn on the idea of an 'allegory of movement' as a broad descriptor of the complexities of recovery experience.

This is also applicable to practice in social work and health care in which practitioners must often work with people in situations of extreme uncertainty, in which 'practices are more analogous with art forms of music and dance than the rationalities of conscious thought' (Gunaratnam 2015, p. 7). She cites Deleuze who suggests

> It is by speed and slowness that one slips in among things, that one connects with something else. One never commences; one never has a tabula rasa; one slips in, enters in the middle; one takes up or lays down rhythms.

To borrow from Ingold (2011) we argue that recovery is open-ended: its impulse is not to reach a terminus but to keep on going. The work of FADT, encourages the dancer to launch into a movement, to 'hazard an improvisation'. This is a deconstructed world of care which needs to be approached in its own terms. It is a world understood in terms of affective relationships in a state of constant movement and interchange. Ultimately, and vitally the work of FADT creates a space for each individual's world to join in with the World that we all share.

Acknowledgements

We acknowledge the support and contribution of everyone at Fallen Angels and the support of Tim Lamford from the University of Central Lancashire who supported the analysis of the movement data.

Funding

This work was supported by the Richard Benjamin Trust [grant number RBT 1305].

Note

1. http://www.fallenangelsdancetheatre.co.uk
2. http://www.kcl.ac.uk/ioppn/depts/addictions/Scales,-Measures-and-Instruments/ SURE-Substance-Use-Recovery-Evaluator.aspx

References

Berlant, L. (2011). *Cruel optimism*. Durham, NC: Duke University Press.

Braidotti, R. (2011). *Nomadic theory*. New York, NY: Columbia University Press.

Deleuze, G., & Guattari, F. (1988). *A thousand plateaus*. London: Continuum.

Derrida, J. (1991). Psyche: inventions of the other. In P. Kamuf (Ed.), *A Derrida reader. Between the blinds* (pp. 200–221). New York, NY: Columbia University Press.

Espeland, W. N., & Stevens, M. L. (2008). A sociology of quantification. *European Journal of Sociology, 49*, 401–436.

Froggett, L., Manley, J., & Roy, A. (2015). The visual matrix method: Imagery and affect in a group-based research setting. *Forum Qualitative Sozialforschung/Forum: Qualitative Social Research, 16*. Retrieved from http://www.qualitative-research.net/index. php/fqs/article/view/2308/3849

Gunaratnam, Y. (2015). *Death and the migrant: Bodies, borders and care*. London: Bloomsbury.

Ingold, T. (2007). *Lines: A brief history*. London: Routledge.

Ingold, T. (2011). *Being alive: Essays on movement, knowledge and description*. London: Routledge.

Ingold, T., & Kurtilla, T. (2000). Perceiving the environment in Finnish Lapland. *Body and Society, 6*, 193–196.

Kelly, J. F., Hoeppner, B., Stout, R. L., & Pagano, M. (2012). Determining the relative importance of the mechanisms of behavior change within alcoholics anonymous: A multiple mediator analysis. *Addiction, 107*, 289–299.

Lewis, C. S. (1936). *The allegory of love*. Oxford: Oxford University Press.

Manley, J. (2013). Movement inside, movement outside: The arts, creativity and sport. In D. Sandle, J. Long, J. Parry, & K. Spracklen (Eds.), *Fields of vision: The arts in sport* (pp. 99–119). Eastbourne: LSA Publication No. 125.

Manley, J., Roy, A., & Froggett, L. (2015). Researching recovery from substance misuse using visual methods. In L. Hardwick, R. Smith, & A. Worsley (Eds.), *Innovation in social work research* (pp. 191–211). London: Jessica Kingsley.

Manley, J., & Roy, A. (Forthcoming). Researching recovery from alcohol and substance misuse using visual methods with FADT Dance Theatre. In K. Niven, S. Lewis, & C. Kagan (Eds.), *Social impact: Making a difference with psychology*. London: RBT.

Marks, J. (1998). *Gilles Deleuze: Vitalism and multiplicity*. London: Pluto.

Monaghan, M. & Wincup, E. (2013). Work and the journey to recovery: Exploring the implications of welfare reform for methadone maintenance clients. *International Journal of Drug Policy, 24*, e81–e86.

Neale, J., Panbianco, D., Finch, E., Marsden, J., Mitcheson, L., Roe, D., Strang, J., & Wykes, T. (2016). Emerging consensus on measuring addiction recovery: Findings from a multistakeholder consultation exercise. *Drugs: Education Prevention and Policy, 23*, 31–40.

O'Neill, M. (2014). Participatory biographies: Walking, sensing and belonging. In M. O'Neill, B. Roberts, & A. Sparkes (Eds.), *Advances in biographical methods: Creative applications* (pp. 73–89). London: Routledge.

Roy, A.. (2017, Janaury 17). Recovery as cruel optimism: Exploring recent responses to substance misuse through policy, practice and lived experience. ESRC – complex needs to disordered personalities: Political discourses and practice responses. Vauxhall: The Foundry.

Roy, A. (2016). Learning on the move: Exploring work with vulnerable young men through the lens of movement. *Applied Mobilities, 1*, 207–218.

Roy, A., & Buchanan, J. (2015). The paradoxes of recovery policy: Exploring the impact of austerity and responsibilisation for the citizenship claims of people with drug problems. *Social Policy and Administration, 50*, 398–413.

Rothfield, P. (2011). Dance and the passing moment: Deleuze's Nietzsche. In L. Guillaume & J. Hughes (Eds.), *Deleuze and the body* (Chap. 10, pp. 203–224). Edinburgh: Edinburgh University Press.

Tambling, J. (2010). *Allegory*. London: Routledge.

Tilley, C. (2004). *The materiality of stone: Explorations of landscape phenomenology*. Oxford: Berg. UK Drug Policy Commission. (2008, July). *The UK DPC recovery consensus group: A vision of recovery*. Policy Report. London. Retrieved from www.ukdpc.org.uk/wp-content/uploads/Policyreport-Avisionofrecovery_UKDPCrecoveryconsensusgroup.pdf

Roy and Manley - O'Neill and McHugh

Roy and Manley's paper and O'Neill and McHugh's paper both make the case for a performative praxis in social work, social care and health. Through developing methods based on human movement they show how the internal movement of thoughts and emotions can be understood and communicated through bodily movement. Roy and Manley's paper explores the practice of Fallen Angels Dance Theatre which uses dance workshops and performance to support people in recovery from substance misuse. O'Neill and McHugh's paper is based on a walk with Faye, presenting a photo essay which conveys the complexity of the life of a woman living temporarily in direct access accommodation in a British city. Both papers draw on psychosocial approaches. Roy and Manley's paper uses the Visual Matrix method alongside group-based movement sessions, which together prioritize visualization, association and embodied, affective experiences as part of a group-based exploration. O'Neill describes how her attempt to better understand the lived experience and lived cultures of marginalised groups, led her to develop an approach to participatory research and praxis that she called ethno-mimesis (1999, 2001), a methodology which combines ethnography and the re-presentation of ethnographic data in visual / artistic form, working in collaboration with artists as well as groups and communities. O'Neill and McHugh argue that re-presenting social research in visual / artistic form can provide a richer understanding of the complexity of the lived experiences of people's lives and can also help in taking research to a broader public. The walk taken with Faye from enables a connection with the embodied, emotional, sensory and aesthetic aspects of her everyday life.

O'Neill and McHugh argue that conducting participatory, walking, biographical and arts-based research with individuals and groups promotes purposeful knowledge that may be transformative, accentuating the relationship between thinking, feeling and doing. Both papers (Roy and Manley and O'Neill and McHugh) conclude that people working in social work, social care and health might consider the value of performative praxis, in which embodiment in movement, relationship and affect can support work with vulnerable people.

Maggie O'Neill and Catrina McHugh

WALKING WITH FAYE FROM A DIRECT ACCESS HOSTEL TO HER SPECIAL PLACE IN THE CITY: WALKING, BODY AND IMAGE SPACE. A VISUAL ESSAY

This article shares a walk with Faye, who was living in a direct access hostel, and Open Clasp women's theatre company, to think through the themes of this special edition: the role of vision and imagery in fostering the imagination, 'creative seeing' and creative knowing. As a participatory, arts-based methodology, walking has much to recommend it, especially when combined with visual and biographical forms of research.

Introduction

This photo essay focuses attention on the utter complexity of the life of a woman living temporarily in direct access (DA) accommodation in a British city. In taking a walk with Faye from a place she calls home to a special place in the city, we connect with the embodied, emotional, sensory and aesthetic aspects of her everyday life and subsequently make sense of and share Faye's meanings and experiences here in this photo essay; as well as in Open Clasp's forthcoming play 'Sugar'. We suggest that using walking methods, sociologically, alongside arts-based outcomes and interventions (in this case photography, storytelling and theatre), participatory collaborations between the arts and social research might make a significant contribution to better knowledge and understanding, challenge the stereotypes and the stigma homeless women experience, as well as offer ways of both feeding into practice and policy and social justice, i.e. social work, health work and social care, through performative praxis (O'Neill et al. 2002). In keeping with the philosophy underpinning the walking methods undertaken here, Roy et al. (2015) suggest

> mobile methods are of relevance to social work researchers because harnessing movement and the relationship between humans and place can alter the conditions of knowledge making and uncover new meanings and understandings of people's lives.

Moreover, bringing the experiences of women in temporary DA hostel accommodation "into visibility and recognition" enables the production of "caring encounters" (Roy 2016) and social justice.

Walking biographies: ethno-mimesis as performative praxis

In an attempt to better understand the lived experience and lived cultures of marginalised groups, O'Neill (1999, 2001) developed an approach to participatory research and praxis that she called ethno-mimesis. Ethno-mimesis is defined as a renewed methodology for social research that combines ethnographic research and the re-presentation of ethnographic data in visual/artistic form, working in collaboration with artists as well as groups and communities. Re-presenting social research in visual/artistic form can provide a rich understanding of the many issues surrounding the lived experiences of women: challenge stereotypes; bring the work to a wider audience; develop public understanding and feed into social policy.

The concept of Ethno-mimesis, (influenced by Benjamin and Adorno's use of 'mimesis') privileges the inter-relationship between the psychic and social processes involved in the process of participatory, collaborative, co-produced research and art making. Inspired by artists who use walking as part of their practice, O'Neill includes walking in her ethno-mimetic practice. Walking[1] illuminates the researcher's self-reflexive involvement in the research, including being immersed in a physical and emotional/psychic sense in the lived cultures and mobilities of the individuals and groups who are the co-creators of the research. However, for the researcher, immersion in 'lived cultures' is necessarily accompanied by the creation of the necessary space, or critical distance for interpretation, commentary, critique and narrative/meaning making.

As an artist, writer and director who undertakes ethnographic research from a feminist perspective to produce theatre that makes a difference, that is change making, McHugh (2016) highlights the importance of working with women [not on or for]. She describes feeling her way into their lives with them, using storytelling and interactive theatre methods in workshops where characters are drawn and developed through the stories told by the women. The script for the play is formed in the space between immersion in women's lives and stories and the creative, mimetic process of the writing, an example of co-producing a script that enables women's voices to speak and be heard. Open Clasp's[2] theatre-making is rooted in the lives and experiences of women, for example women experiencing violence, prison, migration, care work and poverty, homelessness.

Methodologically, this process of conducting participatory, arts-based and biographical research is similar in both O'Neill and McHugh's work. O'Neill has conducted participatory action research with communities for most of her career as an academic and the majority of the research projects have been conducted in collaboration with artists and community arts organisations, taking a biographical approach, that often involves walking as part of the method.

A central element of McHugh's practice is to lead workshops where women feel safe to communicate their thoughts and feelings in relation to issues that have impacted on their lived lives. The process is collaborative and democratic. Interactive drama techniques get women moving, creating scenes that mimic their real-life experiences. The scenes or images that are created give individuals an opportunity to stand back and observe their life experiences, significant turning points and the impact issues such as domestic violence and abuse have on their lives. As a biographical and performative method, using the drama techniques enables people to tell and see their stories physically, materially in action, and their words played back to them, enable a space for recognition and reflection. Individuals take risks in doing this and are supported by experienced actors. This takes courage, confidence and self-esteem that are gained through the process.

> The women we work with are the change-makers, they invest their time, take risks and stand tall. They are heroes, they survive experiences that no one should ever have to and many wouldn't be able to. Open Clasp meets these women as equals, standing in solidarity and together we make change happen (McHugh 2016).

In May 2016, McHugh and Open Clasp Theatre set up residency in a Women's DA hostel that provides emergency accommodation for women who are homeless. For six evenings, they met with the women in the hostel's canteen, ending each session by sitting round a table and eating a cooked meal, provided by dedicated hostel staff, that supported the project to happen. Some of the women attended every session, others, pulled by the smell of cooked food, joined the sessions as they concluded; others joined us in the middle of a session. Open Clasp collaborated with 21 women in total.

O'Neill joined the theatre workshop, bringing her walking biographical method into the process[3] taking the women and practitioners out into the city in a two-day walk shop.

As researchers, writers and in McHugh's case a play write and actor, the similarities in approach and method involve immersion in the women's lives, through their narratives and workshop activities and a reflective, feeling engagement, '*a politics of feeling*' (O'Neill 2001) that highlights the importance of connecting individual experience, 'private troubles', with societal relationships and structures by engaging with the creative, sociological imagination (Wright Mills 2000).

Theatre and walk shop

Open Clasp's participatory approach means that ordinary women take part in the production of theatre and this often changes their lives as well as the lives of audiences who attend the plays. The process involves talking to experts, reading the available literature and working with women, as a social researcher would, in both 1–1 and shared group workshops. The women help to create the characters in workshops and the storyline emerges through these interactions. Hence, Open Clasp's innovative model of working is an example of *ethno-mimesis* and *a politics of feeling* in action: participatory, collaborative research with marginalised women and young women, using transformative theatre-based methods as social engagement and social research and rigorous ethical practice. The stories and narratives of the women are woven into the script and play, the narrative scaffolding and storylines develops in the workshop.

The women draw upon their own experiences to create a character, in this case, the women developed a character called *Tracy*. Often, new women joining would ask "who's Tracy?", and then start to share their own stories that led to them being in the hostel. All the women saw the hostel as a place of safety and were extremely grateful for the provision.

On Thursday evening, O'Neill met the women and *Tracey*, took part in the discussions and drama-based activities and introduced the idea that the following day we would map a walk and then walk together. During the 'walk shop', women were first asked to draw a map from the DA hostel, or a place they called home, to a special place, marking the landmarks along the way that are important to them, for whatever reason.[4] We discussed each map with each woman and recorded our conversations.

The following maps give a sense of some of the women's lives and lived experiences, their routes and mobilities and in one case the very small space she feels safe enough to 'be' in.

Draw a map from a place you call home to a special place

A number of women sat with us at the table and created maps. One woman talked us through her map and what it meant to her, although she did not want to walk. Her special place was Styal prison, where she felt safe. When she was 'thrown out' she slept under bridges and in the park. She placed a cross in the centre of the park, this is where she was raped. She tells us that she was too proud to tightly wrap her sleeping bag around her and that she covered her identity as a woman in layers and hid her hair. In the DA hostel, she was getting support to stay off drugs and spent some time caring for her sister who was not yet ready to do so. She was a bright and funny woman with a quick wit and expressed such warmth and care for others in the group. Another, young woman, drew a map of a house and garden, with a woman looking out of an upstairs room. The image tells a story of isolation and fear, her space circumscribed to the upstairs room, looking out at garden and the garden path leading to a fragment of sunshine in the far-left corner of the page.

Faye's map and walk

Faye drew a map from the DA Hostel to her special place, the park, through the areas where she works, the dark tunnels and the passing cars, past the special tree she touches for luck, the outreach organisation that offers support, care, comfort and practical necessities; and she talked about the split second decisions she makes as to whether she should step into a car with a stranger. Along the way, Faye shared some of her biography and journeys with us, the violent Father, the Mother who left him with the children, the boarding school she was sent to, to stop her absconding, the eight GCSE's, her love of music, singing and drama and the missing years, the people she has lost, how life has passed her by and her fear of being alone.

At the end of the walk, we sat in the park gardens, drinking 'posh' coffee and going back to the beginning of her life, to the child who was invited into a car, given £20, and who then was able to buy batteries for her Walkman. A child hit hard, and a mother that closed the door behind her. We talked about her aspirations, her wants and desire to change, to live and have a good and happy life, against the tide of her life, a tide that comes towards her, over and underneath her, often taking her feet away from her. Faye said she had a good voice and she has, she sang a fragment from a favourite song to us:

> Hold you in my heart, your love is king, never be apart, your kisses ring round and round and round my head touching the very heart of me making my soul sing I'm crying out for more, your love is king.

Faye led the walk, she was in 'situational authority' (see Myers 2007). We were able to connect, see and feel with Faye in an embodied way. Attuning to Faye, her routes through a particular geography of the city, focused our attention on the material as well as the sensory, affective dimensions of her lived experience and the relationship between the visual and other senses. In this sense, O'Neill and Hubbard (2010) have argued that walking is relational, embodied and revelatory; it opens a dialogue and a space where embodied knowledge, experience and memories can be shared (Ingold & Lee Vergunst 2008; O'Neill 2014; O'Neill & Perivolaris 2015; Solnit 2001). Using similar visual methods, 'photo-production' Radley, Hodgetts, and Cullen (2005) and Radley, Chamberlain, Hodgetts, Stolte, and Groot (2010) have helped to visualise homelessness through people's photographs and stories of their lives in hostels and on the streets, analysed in relation to concepts of exclusion, estrangement and survival with walking, "as means, as condition and as occasion" (Radley et al. 2010, p. 36). Similarly, from a 'mobilities' (Urry 2007) perspective Smith and Hall (2016) discuss the ways that outreach workers, work on the move, from the office, in city spaces, searching for the clients to provide care and support for homeless people in the city centre.

On the final day of the workshop, Faye presented the walk back to the other women. Her walk was shared as an exhibition, she wrote on the back of each photograph, a comment and/or a short story about the places that are important to her. There was huge pride and a shared recognition in the room amongst other sex workers of the journey they take each day, and the lives that have led to this moment, to the hostel, to the sore legs and bleeding eyes, the laughter and hope for change.

Methodologically, the walk acted as a holding space/'potential space' (Winnicott 2005) for fragments of Faye's biography to emerge in the discursive, relational and intersubjective recognition occurring between us on the walk and then told again in the relationship between storytelling, photographic images and theatre-making with the whole group.

Although we recorded the conversation along the walk with Faye from the DA hostel to her special place in the city centre, the narrative we share below was created by Faye as she prepared each photograph to be placed on the wall with her map.

Faye chose certain photographs and talked us through the significance and meaning of each place to her, documenting her narrative on the back of each photograph and then placing the photos around her map on the wall. Faye's walk and narrative, the images, maps and sound files will contribute to the developing storyline, script and characters of 'Sugar' together with the character of Tracy crated by women taking part in the residency with Open Clasp.

We hope that this will also contribute to the literature on sex work and homelessness and social work practice. The benefits of working in participatory ways using the arts are that they can help to claim a space for voice, raise awareness of relations of marginalisation, exclusion as well as inclusion and challenge exclusionary processes and practices. Arts-based methods can support the articulation of stories of identities, strength, resilience and belonging for those situated in the in-between spaces of cities. Such methods are vitally important to the creation of dialogue around women's issues and needs, recognition that also challenge the reduction in services and support for women. Ultimately, they reinforce cultural citizenship and promote social justice for women.

The visual essay below by Faye gives readers an insight into her biography and the lives of women living in the DA hostel. We hope that telling this story may move official listeners and enable others to connect with and better understand women's lives.

Body and image space: interactive theatre and walking methods for social justice

In this photo essay, we gain an insight into and understanding of the intersection of human biography and history (micrology) that reveals the public issues behind personal troubles. Such understanding can contribute to practice as well as theory. *Bilddenken*, or thinking in images, and its relation to the body are central to Walter Benjamin's work (Benjamin 1985, 1992). Faye uses a combination of 'body and image space' (Weigel 1996) in telling her story, which is also, in part, a biography of the city and homelessness.

One of the issues that emerged during the walk is the visual prevalence of homelessness, the images of tents in the city centre where people are sheltering, sleeping and living. The walk drew our attention to this, as a broader public issue, writ large in the Faye's images and text. We talked about why we walk past 'tent city' and why this is acceptable in 2017.

Mestrovic (1997) introduced the concept of *post emotional society* in the context of contemporary 'me dominated', and media-saturated society where spaces to think and feel critically are diminishing; and where there is a degree of pessimism and paralysis in our responses to the crisis and plight of others. This paralysis is a marker of post emotionalism. We turn the page, switch off – unmoved. Mestrovic draws upon Adorno's thesis regarding the growth and power of the culture industry in helping to create and sustain an almost totally administered society, where spaces to think and feel critically are constantly diminishing. However, for Adorno, creativity, art and creative production are potentially transformative: "art, is a refuge for mimetic behaviour. It represents truth in the twofold sense of preserving the image of an end smothered completely in rationality and of exposing irrationality and absurdity of the status quo" (Adorno 1984, p. 79).

As an arts-based participatory methodology, walking has much to recommend it, especially when combined with ethnographic, visual and biographical forms of doing research. Walking methods can help articulate the phenomenological, lived, embodied and imagined yet transitory sense of being and belonging as well as giving priority to walking and thinking as 'body and image-space' as a means of 'modulating alienation' as well as 'that crucial element of engagement of the body and the mind with the world, of knowing the world through the body and the body through the world' (Solnit 2001).

In re-presenting women's lives in visual/artistic and performative form, we can express the complexities of lived experience include the material, the sensory and the affective, and what Adorno alludes to as the 'unsayable', those aspects of lived experience that are hard to put into words.

One way of showing how this operates in action is with reference to the way that through walking with women, the photo essay below and making theatre can come into being in the *performance*, i.e. in listening in an active sense to women's stories, attuning to women's everyday routes and in imagining characters and storylines with them, not in a superficial way, but in a deeply engaged way. Working with women in participatory ways, creating images, stories and theatre, based upon their narratives can offer resistance, action and transformation.

For McHugh and O'Neill (as researchers, writers and artists), immersion in 'lived cultures' is necessarily self-reflexive involving the dialectical exploration of lived experience and lived cultures to facilitate the re-presentation of women's lives in visual, poetic, artistic and theatre-based forms.

The inter-textuality between ethnographic research, walking and artistic re-presentation illuminates the complexity of women's lives through what Taussig (1993) alludes to as 'sensuous knowing'. However, this is always in tension with reason and rationality or critical thinking. Not to give oneself over, or to 'project' oneself onto the work but to hold a space for critical reflection, for a radical democratic imaginary, for social justice to emerge.

In the following section, we share our walk with Faye through her images and text (Figures 1–10).

FIGURE 1 Walking with Faye: from Direct Access to a special place. Image: Maggie O'Neill.
First official experience here at DA. This is the reception. I'd like to note the protective screen. Newcomers would think of violent residents, because I did wonder why it was in place.

FIGURE 2 The walk starts at the front desk. Image: Faye.
The door of salvation, because no matter what you think of the place, no one can enter to hurt you. Once you are in you are safe. The long path hopefully ending the long journey of other kinds. A 'finally here' feeling.

FIGURE 3 Front door of the hostel. Image: Faye.
The car park that is crossed, it's behind a derelict block of flats. Shame as I see it being a lovely place. This is a place for dealers and the girls to wait. It's worth pointing out that the meeting place borders a school that is often full of children playing outside.

FIGURE 4 The car park is a lovely place. Image: Faye.

The Apollo roundabout is an important focal point to the entire story really, each turn off represents nine times out of ten what a person in this (kind of) life what they are doing, grafting, using, scoring … from here you can go to DA, you can go to buy drugs, you can go to the red-light area, you can go to tent city so this is like the middle bit from here, that roundabout does represent something in each direction.

FIGURE 5 The Apollo roundabout. Image: Faye.

The walk to the beat brings you to shady spots, especially at night it looks totally different. The place I always take a deep breath and think here we go I hope it's over soon. Although it (the beat) extends further..I always feel that I have reached work at this point.

FIGURE 6   Walking towards the beat. Image: Maggie O'Neill.

The first time I ever did sex work was by accident, I was only very young I was fifteen and I'm forty-one now. I had my very first twenty-pound note, he just gave me just to sit in his car for ten minutes. I loved it, that was it, I was gone. I bought loads of batteries for my Walkman. I like old school soul music. I was very lucky because I was never abused like you know like not strangers but my dad was very violent and I had some near misses with my life when I was at home.

FIGURE 7   My favourite tree. Image: Faye.

Each day I go to work I have to walk across the roots of this beautiful old tree and I thank it for allowing me to walk over its legs.

FIGURE 8   Red light. Image: Faye.
A quiet or intimidating view of the back streets of this red-light area, this is in the day – a haven when it rains, god knows I hate this place.

FIGURE 9   A special place. Image: Faye.
Walking towards the gardens we pass Tent City. Tent City for street homeless is across the road, the homeless often find themselves spending time in one of these set ups. I can only imagine what happens here.

FIGURE 10   Sharing my walk. Image: Maggie O'Neill.
A shot of the gardens where our journey paused for posh coffee ☺ Deep in conversation as we were all day.

Discussion

Walking with Faye reinforced the experience of walking as (relational, revelatory, sensory and embodied) in the borders and margins of the city, the alleyways, back spaces, underpasses, the 'red light' area to reach the city centre and the gardens. Through Faye's walk, we attuned to her story, her experiences and reflections on border spaces and places both real and imagined in a sensory way and connected to her bravery and resilience and search for belonging as feeling/being in place and at home, albeit 'on the move.'

The walk shops and theatre workshops were underpinned by the principles of participatory action research. They were spaces to share stories, experiences, meanings, mobile lives and conduct the critical interpretive analysis required for sharing the research findings in both this essay form and the form of theatre. Through the workshops, participants told their stories through a character of their creation, Tracy, exploring what life events and circumstances lead women to these experiences, what services for women dealing with these issues are like and how society treats them. The women also say what they would like audiences to understand about their lived experiences.

The feedback from women involved in the long history of Open Clasp's theatre workshops on these issues is consistently positive and speak of growing confidence, thinking through barriers and support and also recognising their gifts; elements that can often take second place to the daily chaos of being on the move, being poor, selling sex, dealing with the aftermath of historic or recent sexual abuse, exploitation and/or domestic violence.

The photo essay was produced in the context of a walk shop as one part of a theatre workshop and residency and is a biographical as well as a social document of the history in which it is produced. It may also be read as a micrology an example of where "the splinter in your eye is the best magnifying glass" that calls us to reflect upon, challenge and transform the sexual and social inequalities in evidence here, towards social justice for women.

Moving out of the DA Hostel, sharing a walk with Faye from a place she called home to a special place enabled us as researchers and theatre practitioners to get to know Faye's lived experiences, her routes and mobilities in action. Taking a walk with Faye enabled a way of knowing and thinking that is done on the move, in a connected, embodied and relational way. The implications for creative practice and social work practice are clear, as Hughes, Roy and Manley (2014), Roy et al. (2015) and Ferguson (2016) have evidenced.

Conducting participatory, walking, biographical and arts-based research with individuals and groups promotes purposeful knowledge that may be transformative, and certainly counter's paralysis and pessimism. The relationship between thinking, feeling and doing (Arendt 1970), commitment and collective responsibility is central to our respective and combined research as well as our creative practice [theatre and walking], and has the following outcomes.

First, for welfare practitioners, hostel key workers and social workers, walking with service users as a central element of 'practice' can facilitate "the kind of client-centred knowledge needed not only to understand individual stories of survival, but also inform appropriate and timely practice interventions" (Roy et al. 2015, p167). Roy et al. (ibid) argue that "mobile methods are of relevance to social work researchers" because they not only harness "movement and the relationship between humans and place can alter the conditions of knowledge making and uncover new meanings and understandings of people's lives" but also "social work and welfare practices are founded on mobilities". Ferguson (2016), extends this point by evidencing how social work is a form of work on the move that "takes place in a whole range of different sites and settings" (p. 195). Practitioners move between the different areas of practice, are co-present with service users, and this gives rise to praxis – as purposeful knowledge.

Second, the recursive relationship that evolves in practice and in research using mobile methods, between theory, lived experience and praxis (as purposeful knowledge) can give rise to and facilitate interventions in practice and policy – and may have real impact as a consequence of the mobile, attuned, embodied and creative methods used.

Third, from this mobile, phenomenological approach, we experience meaning making on the move that enhances awareness of the relationship, between private troubles, biography and societal relationships and structures; challenging hegemonic thinking and enabling us to brush history against the grain, to promote social justice.

Taken together these three points also impact on the possibilities for a radical democratic imaginary in the twenty-first century (see also Back 2007; Froggett & Hollway 2010; O'Neill 2009; O'Neill & Seal 2012) connecting walking, performative, and mobile methods 'body and image space' to social action. In *Transgressive Imaginations: crime, deviance and culture* O'Neill and Seal close the book with an invitation to develop an agenda for a transgressive, radical democratic imaginary drawing upon Bauman (2011). This invitation is as relevant today as it was in 2012 and (following Bauman) we need research into practice that serves to:

(i) de-familiarise the familiar and familiarise the unfamiliar. Bauman (2011) made reference to Milan Kundera's call for artists and the humanities and social sciences to join forces. We argue that arts-based mobile methods including walking methods and theatre can help to achieve this.

(ii) 'only connect', take up interaction with other spheres of human life, show the interconnections. The inter-disciplinary, mobile, participatory, biographical methods can develop connections, chains of signification across theory and practice but also across disciplines, art, social work, criminology, sociology, biography, theatre studies. Developing knowledge in partnership *with* the stereotypical subjects of research can facilitate connections that make a difference.

(iii) 'unravelling doxa' – 'knowledge with which you think but of which you don't know'. Unravel "the prevailing view of things" (Merrick 2006). This is synonymous with ideology critique, critical thinking and reflexivity. Researchers and practitioners "need to concern ourselves not only with the art of thinking, but the art of listening and seeing too" (O'Neill & Seal 2012, p. 158). Using innovative methodologies in research and practice, using 'body and image space' is vital to the art of thinking critically and creatively for developing and sustaining a 'radical democratic imaginary'.

(iv) open and keep open dialogue. In our research and practice we aspire to "dialogue that is interdisciplinary/transdisciplinary, that fosters mutual trust, and subject–subject relationships as far as possible – which values expertise in communities, uncovers hidden histories, shares knowledge and expertise" (O'Neill & Seal 2012, p. 158) as well as the highest quality of research and practice. Opening and keeping open spaces to think critically, to inform theory, policy and practice is vital to envisioning social justice, in this case with homeless women, sex workers and welfare and housing practitioners.

We leave the last word to Faye who tells us:

If I could do anything I'd like to be a support worker you know and like work with young people and try to sort of make sense of it with them. But you know, I just sometimes think that I don't know who to reach out to get a life, I want to establish myself as a person because I'm just like, I feel I'm just floating between situations at the minute and I don't know what's going to happen to me, it's scary. I just want to be productive, I don't want to just exist.

Acknowledgement

We thank Direct Access Hostel for Women, the key support worker, Tricia Duffy and Faye.

Funding

This work was supported by the Leverhulme Trust [grant number RF 2015 316].

Notes

1. Walking methods are gaining ground in social science research (Clark & Emmel 2010; Edensor 2010; Pink 2007; Pink et al. 2010; Urry 2007). O'Neill's approach to walking was inspired initially by walking women artists, the work of Tim Ingold, anthropologists, as well as the aforementioned social scientists. For their application within social work see Roy (2016), Roy (this edition), Hughes, Roy, and Manley (2014), Roy, Hughes, Froggett, and Christensen (2015) and Ferguson (2016)

2. Open Clasp is a multi-award-winning women's theatre company seen as exemplars in their field with a proven track-record of success spanning 18 years. Founded in 1998, they are based in the north-east of England and have a national and international reach. Open Clasp unique approach and practice, sees them collaborating with women on the margins of society to create exciting theatre for personal, social and political change. Their work is directly informed by the lived experiences of the women and young women they collaborate with and rooted in the belief that theatre changes lives. Open Clasp are committed to working in partnership and sharing good practice in the field of participatory theatre, engaging with policy-makers providing vital first-hand research, evaluation and recommendations.

3. As part of her Leverhulme fellowship. The fellowship focuses upon using walking methods to understand borders, risk and belonging and to explore the method of walking to conduct research that is arts-based, participatory and collaborative. See: www.walkingborders.com.

4. Following Myer's (2007) art practice. See also O'Neill (2014), Myers (2010) and O'Neill and Hubbard (2010).

References

Adorno, T. (1984). *Aesthetic theory*. London: Routledge and Kegan Paul.

Arendt, H. (1970). *On Violence*. New York, NY: Harcourt Publishing Company.

Bauman, Z. (2011). *Reflections on Economy and Society*. Presentation to the University of Durham: School of Social Sciences.

Back, L. (2007). *The art of listening*. London: Berg.

Benjamin, W. (1985). *One way street and other writings*. (E. Jephcott & K. Shorter, Trans.). London: Verso.

Benjamin, W. (1992). *The storyteller, in Illuminations*. (H. Zohn, Trans.) (pp. 83–107). London: Fontana Press.

Clark, A., & Emmel, N. (2010). *Using walking interviews*. Manchester: Morgan Centre, University of Manchester.

Edensor, T. (2010). Walking in rhythms: Place, regulation, style and the flow of experience. *Visual Studies, 25*, 46–58.

Ferguson, H. (2016). Professional helping as negotiation in motion: Social work as work on the move. *Applied Mobilities, 1*, 193–206. doi:10.1080/23800127.2016.1247523

Froggett, L., & Hollway, W. (2010). Psychosocial research analysis and scenic understanding. *Psychoanalysis, Culture and Society, 15*, 281–301.

Hughes, J., Roy, A., & Manley, J. (2014). *Surviving in Manchester: Narratives on movement from the Men's Room*. Preston: University if Central Lancashire.

Ingold, T., & Lee Vergunst, J. (2008). *Ways of Walking: Ethnography and Practice on Foot*. London: Routledge.

McHugh, C. (2016). *Changing the world one play at a time* Retrieved from https://openclasp.wordpress.com/

Merrick, D. (2006). *Social work and child abuse: Still walking the tightrope?* London: Routledge.

Mestrovic, S. G. (1997). *Postemotional society*. London: Sage.

Myers, M. (2007). Along the way: Situation-responsive approach to education and participation. *International Journal of the Arts in Society, 1* (2), 1–6.

Myers, M. (2010). Walk with me, talk with me: The art of conversive wayfinding. *Visual Studies, 26*, 50–68.

O'Neill, M. (1999). *Adorno, culture and feminism*. London: Sage.

O'Neill, M. (2001). *Prostitution and feminism: Towards a politics of feeling*. Cambridge: Polity Press.

O'Neill, M., Giddens, S., Breatnach, P., Bagley, C., Bourne, D., & Judge, T. (2001). Renewed Methodologies for social research: ethno-mimesis as performative praxis. *Sociological Review, 50*, 70–88.

O'Neill, M. (2009). Making connections: Ethno-mimesis, migration and diaspora. *Psychoanalysis, Culture & Society, 14*, 289–302.

O'Neill, M. (2014). Participatory biographies: Walking, sensing, belonging. In M. O'Neill, B. Roberts, & A. Sparkes (Eds.), *Advances in biographical methods*. London: Routledge.

O'Neill, M., & Perivolaris, J. (2015). A sense of Belonging: walking with Thaer through migration, memories and space in Crossings. *Journal of Migration & Culture, 5*, 327–338.

O'Neill, M., Giddens, S., Breatnach, P., Bagley, C., Bourne, D., & Judge, T. (2001). Renewed methodologies for social research: Ethno-mimesis as performative praxis. *The Sociological Review, 50*, 69–88.

O'Neill, M., & Hubbard, P. (2010). Walking, sensing, belonging: Ethno-mimesis as performative praxis. *Visual Studies, 25*, 46–59.

O'Neill, M., & Seal, L. (2012). *Transgressive Imaginations*. London: Palgrave.

Pink, S. (2007). Walking with video. *Visual Studies, 22*, 240–252.

Pink, S. Hubbard, O'neill, M., & Radley, A. (2010). Walking across disciplines: from ethnography to arts practice. *Visual Studies, 25* (1), 1–7.

Radley, A., Chamberlain, K., Hodgetts, D., Stolte, O., & Groot, S. (2010). From means to occasion: Walking in the life of homeless people. *Visual Studies, 25*, 36–45.

Radley, A., Hodgetts, D., & Cullen, A. (2005). Visualizing homelessness: A study in photography and estrangement. *Journal of Community & Applied Social Psychology, 15*, 273–295.

Roy, A. (2016). Learning on the move: Exploring work with vulnerable young men through the lens of movement. *Applied Mobilities, 1*, 207–218.

Roy, A., Hughes, J., Froggett, L., & Christensen, J. (2015). Using mobile methods to explore the lives of marginalised young men in Manchester. In L. Hardwick, R. Smith, & A. Worsley (Eds.), *Innovations in social work research* (pp. 153–170). London: Jessica Kingsley.

Solnit, R. (2001). *Wanderlust: A history of walking*. London: Verso.

Smith, R., & Hall, T. (2016). Pedestrian circulations: Urban ethnography, the mobilities paradigm and outreach work. *Mobilities, 11*, 497–507.

Taussig, M. (1993). *Mimesis and alterity: A history of the senses*. London: Routledge.

Urry, J. (2007). *Mobilities*. Cambridge: Polity.

Weigel, S. Z. (1996). *Body- and image-space: Re-reading Walter Benjamin*. (G. Paul, R. McNicholl, & J. Gaines, Trans.). London: Routledge.

Winnicott, D. W. (2005). *Playing and reality*. London: Routledge.

Wright Mills, C. (2000 [1959]). *The sociological imagination*. Oxford: Oxford University Press.

O'Neill and McHugh - Malone

O'Neill and McHugh, Roy and Manley and Malone each make the case for the specialist input of arts professionals. However, whist O'Neill and McHugh and Roy and Manley are social scientists collaborating with arts professionals, Eloise Malone reports on a project led by a small arts organisation working collaboratively with a children's charity on a project exploring the lived experience of Child Sexual Exploitation. The very title of Malone's article makes immediate use of the power of the visual image that we foreground in this Special Edition. From the start we expect truth to be cold, art to be a fulcrum, there will be considerations of recovery, participation, change. The article does not disappoint as it conveys work with and by vulnerable young men and women aged 15-18 with experience of child sexual exploitation (CSE). The article describes how 'high culture' can be understood and made accessible to vulnerable and disadvantaged individuals and groups (much as the recently-deceased David Bowie achieved to such widespread and memorable effect). The young people involved in this work were taken to see works of Art in various galleries and were given some training as artists and curators. Key ideas were established by way of non-linear methods which included play, games, creativity and social dreaming. This process culminated in the creation of a 'mausoleum' of glass-cast and ice-cast children's shoes which slowly fell to pieces throughout each day in the gallery.

Coming from an arts background Malone is especially interested in the transformative power of the art object itself — as well as the accompanying process of involvement in its production. Her central argument is that it is the quality of the art work or curating produced by the young people in these socially engaged arts processes that matters in the sense that it created not only a 'third' through which to think about their experience, but a third with form and quality which in itself communicates something that is distinctive but can be shared. It is this that creates the opportunity for social and civic change through public engagement. This emerges because high quality artistic expression elicits an empathic response from the audience, creating an immediate strong reaction, and a lasting resonance. Malone acknowledges that creation is a necessary but insufficient condition in achieving change. The transformative power of an art object is described in language for 'non-arts specialists' that enables them to appreciate the quality of a created arts object. Those viewing the work were given wired headsets which provided a looped soundtrack to the show. This device thus made use of (also) transitory and yet repeated sound as a means of accentuating what the audience were seeing. The work was arranged so that those viewing it did so by walking over text written on the floor. The shoes the audience were looking at were melting before their eyes while their own shoes remained intact and 'walked over' important information. Plinths were arranged to emulate a war cemetery and lighting was carefully employed to accentuate the effect. Freud's concept of 'The Uncanny' and Jung's writing on archetypes are applied to the work. This is a powerful piece which shows how careful thinking behind conceptual art can produce a visual response to a topic which resonates more forcefully than 'a thousand words'. The young people involved in the project are shown to have benefitted from doing so. One person viewing the work is quoted as saying, "I can't remember the time art moved me as much as The Cold Truth: powerful, heart-breaking, and real." If the impact of work described here were more widely appreciated or understood by commissioners — the implication might be making fuller use of artist and curators in services for children and young people.

Eloise Malone

THE COLD TRUTH: ART AS FULCRUM FOR RECOVERY IN PARTICIPANTS AND FOR CIVIC CHANGE

This article describes art curating with sexually exploited young people. It reviews The Cold Truth: an exhibition produced by CSE survivors at Radiant Gallery, Plymouth, UK, 2016. The article proposes that the quality of the art produced by young people can catalyse social and civic change through public engagement and service commissioner adoption; and a pathway to psychosocial recovery for participants. It examines the transformative power of the art object created during the intervention. The article draws on Frogett et al's "Aesthetic Third" to propose artwork as a fulcrum between silenced children, and communities which avoid unpalatable truths. It proposes that artworks eliciting empathetic responses are more powerful than those stimulating sympathetic responses. It offers Matarasso's indicators of great art as language to consider the quality of art created by children, and to advocate that service leaders and commissioners use quality art processes to design and deliver effective services.

Introduction: project context

Effervescent is a social-design/social-arts lab based in Plymouth. We research how high quality cultural activity can catalyse lasting positive social change in people, places and services. We work collaboratively with vulnerable groups to curate and programme Radiant Gallery – the only professional contemporary art gallery in Europe curated solely by children and young people.[1] As opposed to a technical training in using equipment, software or bodies which is the traditional domain of socially engaged work, we place emphasis on creating new thinking strategies and behaviours in our participants, so that change is sustained long after the project has ended. The particular value of this way of working is the lasting impact on wellbeing, education, aspiration and resilience for the children and young people involved.

The process which created The Cold Truth was a risky programme for us. It was the first time the local authority Plymouth City Council had approached us and asked us for outcomes and impact rather than deliverables (such as a theatre performance or film, for example). We used curatorial process to help young people recover from the devastating experiences of sexual exploitation, and to gather their insight into how services for children with their experiences could be more effective.

We were aware from the outset that the subject matter created nervousness in terms of taste and decency, even amongst the services that commissioned the work. We worked with five young people who were referred through Barnardo's[2] BASE (Barnardo's Against Sexual Exploitation) project. Two Barnardo's youth workers worked alongside two Effervescent artist practitioners throughout the entire process. For Barnardos, the opportunity was to test new ways of working more effectively with art and design, and to support young service users to influence local policy and practice. Effervescent wanted to influence how a major children's charity viewed the place of art in its services and how future service design might integrate arts as a core practice.

Young people were recruited through personal invitation via Barnardo's; then a one-to-one meeting with the Effervescent lead artist and a tour of the gallery. Each young person was asked to identify what they wanted to gain from the experience. Many struggled to articulate what they needed for themselves, but all wanted to make a positive difference to other exploited children and young people.

The group were carefully selected as young people who were in later stages of their journey towards sexual safety, and were relatively stable. Notwithstanding their relative stability, the group included young people who were experiencing varying combinations of: suicidal thoughts or recent suicide attempts; self-harming behaviours; unstable care arrangements; bullying at school; early parenthood; flashbacks, nightmares and anxiety attacks; inability or unwillingness to attend school/college; social isolation; difficulties in communicating with and forming positive relationships with family members; poverty; complex relationships with food including hunger, bulimia, refusing to eat, loss of appetite, oracy difficulties, or poor levels of access to good quality food; and using drugs or alcohol. All of the young people involved had experienced severe and prolonged sexual abuse and sexual exploitation. Three had recently experienced long stays in secure foster care or secure mental health units. Some had been through judicial processes to take their abusers to court and, for those who had, none of them had had a positive experience, or one that acknowledged the trauma they had endured. We worked with a small group of young people to give them the time and attentiveness they needed to be able to talk about complex and difficult experiences in a "held" and safe environment.

Intensive devising: training in art, design and curatorial procedure

We worked with the group from 10 am until 4 pm each day for an initial two weeks. This process allowed us to support the group to form and norm, (Tuckmann cited in Cole 2000), and to begin to research CSE both generally through desk-based research and through sharing lived experiences between the participants. During this intense period, we began training the young people as artists and curators. We visited Plymouth Museum and Hauser & Wirth Gallery in Somerset, to look at artefacts, contemporary art and to discuss curatorial strategies. We created micro-art installations in the corridors, car parks, toilets and studios at Radiant Gallery, and then critically analysed the art works together from the perspective of technique, emotional impact and conceptual content for audiences. Through playful games, creative tasks, social dreaming matrices (Lawrence 2010) and projection/ role play tasks, we assembled key ideas and themes that the participants wanted to communicate in order to begin a public conversation about CSE in Plymouth. We didn't do this by directly asking their opinions on what they wanted to communicate, but through a non-linear method by which we collaboratively "banked" material generated subconsciously through playfulness, and then as a group identified the content that felt most relevant.

Throughout their period of playful devising, the group constantly "played" with written text on the walls of the corridors, with water and ice, with images of shoes arranged in windows and in corners of the room. These were images and symbols which the group naturally kept returning to. There were other images which emerged and which were also strong: an angel in a trashcan, smashed hearts, "wrong" and displaced brides, talking foxes, games of chance, panic buttons, treats which turned out to be cruel tricks. Effervescent core artists who have devised this method of working over nearly 20 years of practice facilitated this playfulness; the method is unique but is similar to a "miniworld" approach sometimes used by play therapists – but played out with the gallery as the mini world, and over days of cumulative training. Effervescent artists devised the process, but the content was populated by the young people in the same way that an inkblot might be created in play and then interpreted by the person playing, or a play house might facilitate any number of scenes of happiness, violence, comfort or outrage.

When the group had collated the images that resonated most strongly with them, they found a way to bring together the research they did on CSE with their own priorities for making the public aware of the issue, and the learning they had developed on how art can create sensation and behavioural change in audiences. The young people proposed a visual- and sound-based art installation designed to evoke the fragility of the children experiencing exploitation; the permanence of the damage caused by this abuse; and to draw attention to the percentage of children who don't seek help: a "mausoleum" of glass-cast and ice-cast children's shoes which slowly fell to pieces throughout each day in the gallery. The young people ideated the initial concept, and then worked with Effervescent's artistic team to refine the audience experience and to commission ice sculptors, glass artists, a musician, carpenters and a film-maker. The entire process involved around 40 days contact, over a period of July 2015 to February 2016.

The theoretical context

In Playing and Reality, Winnicott proposes a transitional object as liminal space between the infant, the parent and the world. This object holds the space between "the inner psychic reality and the external world" (Winnicott 1997). Froggett et al. (2011) and Froggett and Trustram (2014) develop this theory to describe the object, considered in terms of its intrinsic aesthetic qualities as a symbolic "aesthetic third", a powerful and evocative presence which bridges (and therefore provides an architecture for) the space between the creative intention of the person who "finds", "uses" or "makes" it, and the personal meanings that then become attached to it. In this way members of an audience confer personal significance and meaning on art objects. The aesthetic third as a symbol, as an object packed with emotional, social and cultural reference points, but not as a verbatim reconstruction of one experience or one story, is where the power resides in such an object. It resonates with an audience and creates empathetic response as op-posed to sympathetic response.

This difference between sympathetic and empathetic reaction will be familiar to so-cial care professionals. The power of empathy as a tool for learning and change in a client or subject is deeply documented (Rogers 1951) and is an embodied response. Sympa-thetic responses create a dynamic in which the other person is objectified or pushed away – I feel sorry for you, rather than I feel with you. Sympathetic responses continue the isolation of the client, and elevate the sympathiser to a position of otherness, of feel-ing "sorry for" and therefore of superiority; whereas an empathetic response creates a position of togetherness, equality, and touches the audience with a resonance because it is "recognised" at a deep embodied level as truthful and authentic. I will return to these features of resonance and authenticity in my discussion of artistic quality.

The artefact and its relationship to the imagination

It is helpful to describe in some detail the artwork created by the young people in The Cold Truth exhibition, and to consider the rich texture of the work that was sited in a contemporary art gallery. At the entrance to the gallery audiences were invited to wear wireless headsets that played a looped soundtrack to the show. This had the effect of immediately isolating the audience so that each person experienced the installation in a state of being alone within it. The undetectable loop meant that audiences could join at any time and stay as long as they felt they wanted to without a beginning and end to the soundtrack.

Audiences were guided through a solid 15 foot high "kissing gate" style entry point, which prevented them experiencing the art work until they were already immersed in it. As they walked in, they stepped on text written in white on the floor: "72% of sexually exploited children don't tell anyone" and then they looked up to see the installation. Thus, the audience were carefully managed in their entrance, and in their entrancement.

The installation itself was 50 stark grey plinths, roughly the height of a 7-year-old child, arranged in strictly geometric order in lines with text on each plinth facing the entrance (and glass wall) of the gallery. The plinths were placed around 80 cm apart so that audiences could walk between them. A wider "corridor" in a cross formation run-ning the length and breadth of the gallery bisected the show in both directions.

Fourteen of the plinths had a pair of worn children's shoes cast in glass on top of them. These plinths had a very brief description of the age, gender and recovery (or lasting traumatic impact on) a sexually exploited child, taken from real case files and anonymised. The text font was chosen to resemble British war graves from early twentieth century. The shoes symbolised the fragile but "held" nature of children who were vulnerable but receiving help. The other 36 plinths had the word "unknown" written on the plinth, and a pair of child's shoes, again worn, but cast in ice were placed on the plinth and each day in the gallery the ice decayed, melted and ran down the plinth on to the floor so that audiences walked through the water. These ice shoes stood for the 72% of children not reached or aided. As the show continued over three months, the plinths themselves started to show strain and damage, suggesting the damage which is done not just to a child but the support structures around the child coping – family, friends, community.

The formation of the plinths to emulate a war cemetery creates a powerful set of signified concepts: the mass sacrifice; the deluge of pain; young lives lost; violence and damage enacted through control and power. The gallery was lit with a row of pale blue lights, carefully and precisely spaced in a row at the back of the gallery, so that the audience was initially blinded, the "memorials" seemed to go on infinitely and the shoes and plinths backlit so that text was seen after the overall landscape of the space and the glowing of the glass or ice children's shoes.

The aesthetic third (Froggett and Trustram 2014), a symbolic space filled with meanings, created by the placing of these objects with such care in the space, transported audience members into a different emotional and psychological space. The magic of the work was the shift it created. Audience members, a warm mobile presence, were immersed through sound, vision and space in a seemingly endless moment of frozen "children" who were unable to escape and were slowly decaying. By walking on or over the introductory text on the gallery floor, an evocation of lack of civic care or consideration for these children, and the careless way in which predatory adults had treated them, was created; and in stepping on that text, too, the audience was included in that culpability. As time wore on, the white text that stood for those children became more and more damaged, dirtied and distressed.

No "real life" child was shown. The worn shoes stood both for the innocence and playfulness of childhood and the ruined nature of that state for these children, but also the link to a real life really lived. Freud's das unheimlich (Freud et al. 1917/2003) – the everyday object that is familiar but is rendered uncanny by it's displaced presentation – helps us here. The aesthetic third object/art work holds the conceptual notion of a familiar child (whether it is the self, or a child we know) in the audience, but is also able to be saturated in the idea of permanent and continuing damage. Thus, the work becomes not about feeling sorry for someone else, but about feeling with the child who is damaged: an empathetic response rather than a sympathetic reaction. Presenting fifty different pairs of ballet shoes, wellies, trainers and school shoes in sizes from child size 6 to adult size 10, evoked the idea in the audience that it could be any child, it could have been them, it could be a child in their lives right now.

In his discussion of archetypes, Jung (1944/1953) proposes a number of experiences which are known and common to all people - the apocalypse, the wise man, the angel, the deluge, for example - archetypal events, types and motifs which are recognised at a fundamental and instinctive level, akin to the id level of consciousness, without the need for conceptual consideration and super-ego filtering. We recognise them almost at a subconscious level as deep signifiers of a human experience. In The Cold Truth, the quality of art work – the aural isolation, the cold blue and grey surroundings, the geometric war cemetery, the disintegration and unavoidable destruction of a potent symbol of human childhood, the walking on and through the cold hard facts and watery remains of the "children" who had been abused – was designed to trigger a set of archetypal recognitions – and the ensuing physical and emotional responses – in the audience. Here is the apocalypse. Here is the deluge. The layering of sound, lighting, geometry, disintegrating shoes contributed towards an audience experience that was primarily sensory: embodied, rather than conceptual. Meaning was not teased out through intellectual engagement but routed straight to a subconscious level of recognition felt in the body.

It is important that the work was an aesthetic third object, and not just any object or a poorly developed artwork. Just as with Harlow's work on attachment and the insufficiency of a "wire mother" to offer comfort to nurture a baby monkey (Sylva and Lunt 1982), the aesthetic third object has to be honed and "framed" sufficiently, in a "good enough" way, to create the emotional and conceptual bridge between the audience and the young artists' intentions.

Aristotle argues that affect is "that which leads one's condition to become so transformed that his judgment is affected, and which is accompanied by pleasure and pain" (Classics.mit.edu, 2017, p. 6)

A mixture of pleasure and pain becomes crucial – the transformation of the "world" of the audience in that moment through the immersiveness of the experience and the technical adeptness of the realisation (important in order not to distract by any flaws in its production), create an embodied experience which allows the audience to fully engage with the idea behind the work.

> I can't remember the time art moved me as much as The Cold Truth: powerful, heartbreaking, and real (Phil Gibby, Regional Director, Arts Council England, South West).

One of the most resonant outcomes from The Cold Truth was the level of public and professional attention the show received. It is a known fact that a strong and well-created artwork can help to form opinions or inspire people to take action. For example, the domestic violence storyline in BBC Radio 4's serial The Archers[3] in 2016 had a significant effect on reporting statistics with a 20% uplift reported by helplines[4] and much of that attributed to the radio programme (Siddique and Rawlinson 2017). With The Cold Truth, children who had experienced being protected largely through being silenced or held in secure circumstances, suddenly found a powerful voice and it impacted on commissioners' understanding of what service users could bring to their own service design.

> The [art] work generated … has influenced the Multi Agency Child Sexual Exploitation group, encouraging partners from health, education, police, and social care to include the voice of the most vulnerable children in their service planning and delivery models. This project has changed public perceptions; had a positive

impact on the CYP we work with; profoundly changed our approach to service design to the point where we are now reconsidering what we expect to achieve for children, & how arts can be firmly located within those services (Kerstin Neason, Assistant Director, Barnardo's South West).

All of the young people who started the programme completed it. Attendance was 93%, which was 4 – 5 times what would be average attendance at school or an activity for these very vulnerable young people. A set of bespoke tools developed and used by Barnardo's to measure impact in participants demonstrated that the process increased the "protective behaviours" in participants: young people felt significantly more able to make decisions and voice their opinions or feelings; felt that they were spending their time positively, meaningfully and safely; were increasingly able to smile, play, laugh and have fun; and were able to talk about the trauma they had experienced in a positive way that gave them some relief from emotional and mental pain. Young people were significantly more able to make decisions and voice their opinions or feelings. The process also reduced the "harmful factors" that the participants had routinely engaged in. In particular, the participants self-reported that they had reduced engagement in exploitative or harmful sexual behaviour, and that they reduced their reliance on drugs and/or alcohol as a coping mechanism. Four of the young people enrolled in college immediately after taking part in the first section of the programme.

> Profoundly moving beyond description. My granddaughter has lived experience of CSE. It broke all of our hearts. This project has been so healing for her. Thank you (Louise, 53 years, Young Curator's Grandmother).

> For me, those weeks we were here: they were like therapy for me. I went home being quite different. I carried on at home feeling a lot more confident. I stand up for myself. I used to sit there not saying anything to anyone and now I come in the room and I'm all (gestures jazz hands!). It has taught me a lot about myself. It wasn't even about me but I learned a lot through those exercises and I liked it at the end, when it all started coming together and I realised that the stuff we've done – it's not just pointless crap – it's actually getting you somewhere else, somewhere amazing. It turns out to be a piece of art (Young Curator 16).

Discussion

For professionals not working in the cultural arena as a matter of course, finding helpful tools to consider the quality of arts practices can be challenging. Art is not the same as craft – which is about making pleasing objects using manual skills. This can be a lot of fun and a useful diversion or activity, but in craft activity the intention to convey complex and difficult information is not present. My proposition is that creating itself is not enough; it is honing a high quality artwork and presenting it to the public that is the vector of significant change. Art can provide a non-verbal and often non-conceptual expression that can be received empathetically by an audience, creating an immediate strong reaction, and a lasting resonance.

I hope this distinction will help non-arts professionals to select artistic partners and to articulate their aims and expectations of artistic products in socially engaged practice. Francois Matarasso, an established commentator on socially engaged arts practices, offers a useful set of keys to unlock discussions about quality of art works. At Effervescent, we use these in our practice with children as young as seven when curating and producing work: Is the work resonant? Is the artwork authentic? Does the artwork have a technical proficiency? Is the work ambitious? Is it unique? Is there something about this that is magical? Not all works must have all six of these qualities in order to be successful, but in combination they are incredibly powerful. They are also easy to understand for people new to art criticism, yet they open up complex discussion where it is needed.

In The Cold Truth we see technically adept work which resonated strongly with audiences because of the use of strong symbols and the authenticity of the work – which came across both in the work, and in the way it was "framed" by the art gallery, with information on the walls about who had curated it, and why.

Often, in the past, creative work with children and young people has been used just as an activity, something to occupy children. However, this dearth of ambition in commissioning meaningful activity for children and young people serves to silence them a second time by failing to offer them sufficient financial resources, time and expertise to help them develop a real voice and to produce work of cultural and social value – to be active citizens and to make a difference in the world. More than that, enabling children to create magical, resonant, public works to draw attention to key ideas that the public have not before seen helps make the case for public investment in social care and the future of children who, very often, are silenced and hidden away, viewed as problems to solve and not as valuable members of society.

> Before, when we told our stories, we were seen as liars. Here we got a voice. Effervescent made us feel like people; not some little thug kid that nobody's going to listen to (Sonny Participant, age 16[5]).

The Cold Truth was seen by Barnardo's and by Effervescent as a way to champion young people's voice and recovery, and to reach new audiences. As a result of the project the local authority has started to ask more questions about how to include children's voice more meaningfully in service design and evaluation processes. The methodology is currently being developed ready for a three-year longitudinal study led by Effervescent with Barnardo's and University of Exeter.

The work drew audiences from across the UK with visitors making the journey from as far away as Edinburgh.[6] More exciting than the reach, was the depth of the engagement: audiences felt drawn to write lengthy and highly engaged responses in the gallery visitors' book and to make the connection between the show and social policy:

> I like the work. It raises awareness of the issue of child sexual abuse in an artistic way that is polite and acceptable to the masses. As a victim of more than one perpetrator, the work also infuriates me: comments here say it is "thought provoking" "heartbreaking". Do people know how many victims will spend a life in and out of prison, rehab, homeless, isolated, lonely, unable to form meaningful relationships

and considered the dregs and a drain on society? The alcoholics, smack/crackheads, wasters, losers, prostitutes, yobbos and misfits. It's ok when the victims are still children: people can understand, and try to help. The very same people have a problem with compassion when the children grow up ... (Anonymous gallery visitor, April 2016).

Notes

1. A curator is "the selector and interpreter of works of art for an exhibition ... incorporating producer, commissioner, exhibition planner, educator, manager and organiser" (George 2015).
2. Barnardo's is the largest children's charity in the UK; it supports vulnerable children and their families to lead happier and more fulfilled lives.
3. *The Archers* is the world's longest running radio soap opera. The British production, which has had more than 18,150 episodes, is broadcast on Radio 4, the BBC's main spoken-word channel.
4. There is a long tradition in Britain of telephone "helplines" where people in distress can phone a trained stranger for anonymous support and guidance. Examples include The Samaritans, ChildLine and The National Domestic Violence Helpline.
5. https://youtu.be/6YjpaZ4BJEk
6. Edinburgh to Plymouth is a 1600 km round trip.

References

Classics.mit.edu. (2017). *The Internet classics archive | rhetoric by Aristotle*. [online]. Retrieved Feb 6, 2017, from http://classics.mit.edu/Aristotle/rhetoric.html

Cole, G. A. (2000). *Management: theory and practice*. London: Continuum.

Freud, S., Mclintock, D., & Haughton, H. (1917/2003). *The uncanny*. New York, NY: Penguin Books.

Froggett, L., & Trustram, M. (2014). Object relations in the museum: A psychosocial perspective. *Museum Management and Curatorship, 29*, 482–497.

Froggett, L., Roy, A., Little, R., & Whitaker, L. (2011). *New Model Visual Arts Organisations and Public Engagement*. [online]. University of Central Lancashire, Preston. http://clok.uclan.ac.uk/3055/1/WzW-NMI%20Report%202%20with%20nav%20bar.pdf

George, A. (2015). *The curator's handbook*. London: Thames & Hudson.

Jung, C. G. (1944/1953). *Psychology and alchemy*. Oxford: Routledge.

Lawrence, W. G. (2010). *The creativity of social dreaming*. London: Karnac.

Rogers, C. (1951). *Client-centred therapy* (1st ed.). Boston, MA: Houghton Mifflin Co..

Siddique, H., & Rawlinson, K. (2017). *The Archers: Call to help domestic abuse victims as Titchener trial starts*. [online]. The Guardian. Retrieved January 12, 2017, from https://www.theguardian.com/tv-and-radio/2016/sep/04/the-archers-call-to-help-domestic-abuse-victims-as-titchener-trial-starts

Sylva, K., & Lunt, I. (1982). *Child development, a first course* (1st ed.). Oxford: Blackwell.

Winnicott, D. W. (1997). *Playing and reality*. London: Routledge.

The Internet classics archive | rhetoric By Aristotle. *Classics.mit.edu*. N.p., 2017. Web. 6 Feb. 2017.

Whereas Malone emphasises the space for reflection afforded by a gallery setting William Titley focuses our attention on the 'great outdoors' and the domestic setting. Titley reports on a project with male carers making use of auto-ethnographic methods which draw on the personal diaries he has completed as an artist. He makes use of "seemingly insignificant data" and expands on these so that finer details of crucial aspects of experience are not lost. In this respect his article illustrates and informs the reflective practice required of practising social workers.

Titley describes how a project set up for male carers was originally entitled 'Shed Life Ways' but developed from this to be named, 'Men Who Care'. A narrow boat trip is described, followed by links with the metaphorical resonances of such a trip as community spaces for 'men who care' are considered. Talking about art is shown to offer respite and solace from the demands of caring for a partner with dementia. The reality of 'safeguarding' concerns are acknowledged in the context of valuing the 'everydayness' of essential human contact. Cooking together, listening to music, walking and photography are shown to provide uniting and bonding experiences. Boundaries between personal and professional roles are highlighted when the author describes taking his grandson with him to join in with an activity and also reflects upon what an appropriate response should be when a comment is made which sounds uncomfortably "too near the mark". He describes how living geographically near to people one is working with can have implications for this work. Lists of words were recorded with a view to using these as coming from a wardrobe as part of a mini art installation. The wardrobe is shown to function as a symbol that changes and develops with the passing of time.

The implications for and possible changes resulting from "the company that we keep" at a basic human level are illustrated. Titley stresses the value of "dwelling in things", and suggests looking at them (more subjectively) from the inside rather than considering them (apparently more objectively) from the outside. This article is timely as the reluctance or inability of many men to articulate issues important to their mental health is a topic of much contemporary debate. The author's reflections on the personal implications of the work described offer a useful example of reflective practice in action and illustrates how even (or especially) the "small things" have much to show us if we can find time and space to look.

William Titley

CREATIVE RELATIONS

Reporting about a project with male home carers, this paper presents some of the interactions, which took place between the participants as they got to know each other, becoming part of each other's lives. Presenting information from the artist's personal diaries as someone who has lived in the participating community all his life, he attempts to reveal the importance of seemingly insignificant data by making diary entries after each event and reflecting on them at a later date. These have been selected to compare the similarities between Tim Ingold's descriptions of creativity and Grant Kester's model for a dialogical aesthetic, which highlights key points in the engagement processes of a socially engaged artist. These reflective notes, made while the experiences were still fresh in his mind, help to illustrate the impact not only on the participants but also upon the artist as a participant in the social process.

Introduction

In *Making: Anthropology, Archeology, Art and Architecture* Tim Ingold explores the act of making in the context of the creation of objects and the use of the maker's materials. His descriptions of engaging with materials and the creative processes involved also hold true when working with people and places in a socially engaged art context. Ingold defines two significant approaches to the creative process; morphogenesis, which places 'the maker from the outset as a participant in amongst a world of active materials', and Hylomorphism, when a practitioner imposes 'forms internal to the mind upon a material world …' (Ingold 2013, p. 21).

Grant Kester in his book Conversation Pieces contrasts two kinds of aesthetic; one portraying the modern artist as a genius who produces objects that are experienced through an immediate aesthetic response to that object, and 'a dialogical aesthetic', which 'suggests a very different image of the artist, one defined in terms of openness, of listening, and of a willingness to accept a position of dependence and intersubjective vulnerability relative to the viewer or collaborator' (Kester 2004, p. 110). His chapter on dialogical aesthetics goes a long way to providing a framework for evaluating the work of socially engaged artists, demonstrating that time, ethics, listening, exchange, openness, context, empathy, collectivity, legacy, acknowledging all forms of communication and recognising the artist as participant all come in to play when discussing such work.

Most of Kester's components can also be found in Ingold's descriptions of engagement with materials, and both of them consider materials as having direct connections to the social world around them at the time at which they were made, viewed, found and used. I aim to apply their theories directly to the context of working with people in an attempt to shed light on particular moments in my creative process. I aim to do this by presenting them in the context of Ingold's morphogenetic and hylomorphic approaches, together with Kester's model for a dialogical aesthetic, which highlights critical aspects of socially engaged arts practice.

In this paper, therefore, I use auto-ethnographic methods to present information from my personal diaries as an artist who has lived in the community where the artwork took place all his life. In doing so, I attempt to reveal the importance of seemingly insignificant data by making diary entries after each event and then expanding/reflecting on them at a later date.

Through reporting about a project with male home carers, I'm going to present some of the interactions which took place between myself (as the artist) and the participants as we got to know each other, and became part of each other's lives. The text takes the form of a series of extracts taken directly from my own personal journals followed by a commentary on each. These have been selected to highlight the similarities between Ingold's descriptions of creativity and Kester's model for a dialogical aesthetic, which highlights key points in the engagement processes of a socially engaged artist. These reflective notes, made while the experiences were still fresh in my mind, help to illustrate the impact not only on the participants but also upon the artist as a participant in the social process.

The project came about through collaboration between a local health care organisation, whose aims are to support and connect voluntary carers in Lancashire, and 'Superslowway', which is one of 21 projects in England called Creative People and Places (CCP). The CCPs, funded by the Lottery and the Arts Council England, aim to present opportunities to involve 'more people choosing, creating and taking part in brilliant art experiences in the places where they live' (CCP Website, 2017).

Originally titled 'Shed Life Ways', the proposal by the caring organisation identified a need to engage particularly with male home carers. The case was made that 45% of registered carers are male and that they especially feel isolated and find it difficult to open up to other people. It was proposed to create a shed or sheds for men to hang out in and engage in craft, with the ultimate goal for the group to grow in numbers, become independent and run their group themselves. In fact, the group that was formed shared a workshop and kitchen space with The Canal & Rivers Trust, and the participants became less interested in making a shed, feeling that they didn't need one, and more interested in a new title for their group 'Men Who Care'.

The names of participants have been changed for anonymity.

Diary extract no. 1 – first impressions

It's always a little unsettling going to meet a new group of people and I guess that's just the nature of the unknown. With a decent supply of tea and nibbles, we each chatted about our interests, hobbies, careers and … space. A shed space (not 'shared space' but can be) now occupied by life essentials for absent companions. Absent and yet present, connected electronically and emotionally to the passengers on this journey via mobile technology, a super-fast superhighway on this very super-slow-way.

Football banter and the cost of playing these days soon led to the decoration of cakes in a time when life in miniature laid down well-trodden tracks, from sheds to houses and back again, to the sound of 10 years worth of Scottish Highland Bagpipes.

Cutting across golden carpets flecked with fisherman blues we emerged from deep within tunnels, into the rushes of forward motion, gently pressing ripples at a pace … of … approximately … 5 … miles … per hour.

Where to next, I wondered?

End of diary extract no. 1

I wrote the above text after being introduced to a small of group of five men on a narrow-boat trip on the Leeds and Liverpool Canal. Every few months the local caring organisation arranged activities and day-trips for home carers to find respite from their usual everyday duties. A couple of men on the trip had met before on other organised activities but most, like me had not been acquainted before. Three of the men agreed to meet up with me a month later and we shared some of our life stories. We lost one member to relocation and another to transport issues, leaving just one man and an artist. So there we were … at some kind of beginning. The goal posts had changed, we didn't have a group to work with, we had to try and create one … or perhaps it could be a project about just one man and an artist?

I am the artist and Tony is a man responsible for the care and welfare of his wife, who suffers a variety of debilitating health conditions, often rendering her housebound for days at a time.

This is a story of men and although they are no longer in a boat, they are nonetheless travelling companions. The boat is a suitable metaphor for imagining a group of people moving together through time and space, and the narrow boat itself suggests a particular speed of travel; a pace that allows for reflection on our experiences, our resources and the surrounding terrain.

We rejoin the story many weeks after the boat trip where Tony and I are discussing how we could attract more men to join us. We conjured up images of a future in numbers but more realistically we considered the prospect of travelling alone, just the two of us on 'our' journey. We dreamed of a community space for men who care, and of taking such a space with us on our travels, to engage with other people and to let them know that we exist, and that we care.

Occasionally, a new member John would join us for a brew, bringing with him a voracious appetite for conversation. He looks after his wife 24/7, who is in the latter stages of dementia, which impacts deeply on his own well-being through lack of both sleep and other human contact outside of his home. We reassured him that it's ok to drop in whenever it suits him, and that the group could develop according to all our interests. Just before leaving on his first visit, he made a point of expressing how much he had enjoyed spending time with us, and that he felt much calmer than when he arrived. This change in him was clearly visible, the more we talked about art and life over breakfast, the more relaxed and relieved he appeared to be. It was obvious to Tony who pointed out to me that John was actually in a seriously vulnerable state of mind.

We agreed to keep John's home situation in mind as the weeks went by, meeting over breakfast every Friday morning: talking, listening and listening some more, sharing our hopes for the group; maybe we could create some art, or share a new skill like cooking our favourite food. The conversation led to John inviting us to lunch at his house, and we accepted.

The more I thought about it, the more I started to worry about safeguarding and ethical issues. We were three blokes who didn't really know each other, and yet we had just agreed to meet at one of our houses for lunch. What if something unexpected occurred and everyone got stressed out?

Diary extract no. 2 – Chilli house visit

I was a little anxious at the thought of meeting his partner, I've not experienced the company of someone with dementia before and didn't know what to expect. Would they freak out at having strangers in the house? I drove to John's house with Tony, who didn't seem phased at all and that helped to calm my nerves a little. Besides, as we were travelling over, John sent me a text to say that it would be just us three. I was still nervous though, I guess I'm just not used to house visits. That reminds me, I saw my best mate last week and we haven't had a social for over 10 years, and I haven't seen my brothers and sisters for months.

John encouraged Tony to help with the cooking, they both like to cook, and I volunteered to photograph the whole process for the blog. John seemed tense but that was his usual starting position whenever we got together. In between the cooking stages, John showed us a photo album from the time he spent with his wife's family abroad. He met her in London and they spent a lot of time travelling the world together before she suddenly became ill. He also showed us his military photos, a letter from the Queen, and his decorative cap badges, all proudly displayed on the walls. Once the pan was full of meat, veg and stock, the chilli was left to simmer while we enjoyed the garden; listening to music from the good old days and enjoying views of the local countryside. He is interested in photography and asks me questions about the subject but I rarely get chance to reply before he is off on another enquiry. Back in the kitchen and it's time for a taste. It was way 'too salty' for Tony and I quickly interjected with how much 'I loved all the different textures of the meat and depth of flavour'. I think that was more of me avoiding conflict than a conscious facilitation of the situation.

End of diary extract no. 2

It felt like a real privilege to be invited into John's house and for him to share with us his secret recipe of 'Five Meats Chilli'. He openly shared his life history by talking us through family albums and souvenir collections, all of which indicated a successful military background and a love for travelling on exotic holidays with his beloved family.

The visit to John's house was my first exposure to life as a carer. It was a glimpse into his physical and very personal world. Tony seemed to take it in his stride, while on the other hand; I became aware that I'd not actually been to someone's house (outside of my family circle) for quite some time.

Diary extract no. 3 – a walk in the hills

At our next meeting we went for a walk in the countryside and I took along my four-year-old grandson. He has met John before at a local art event and got on well with him. I thought it would be a good way to lighten the mood, which could get quite intense at times. This was also an opportunity for me to reciprocate the lunch at John's house by sharing an important and precious part of my life.

Tony and I were worried about the length of the walk and I slipped our concerns into the conversation but John didn't seem to notice. I was a little worried about Tony's breathing (him not being the fittest and also an asthmatic) as we headed up the incline on that very hot day. My grandson was happy holding Rovers' (John's dog) leash and then Tony used it to help pull himself up the hill. John guided us to a beautiful spot by the river, perfect for dropping heavy stones in the deepest parts, the challenge being to make the biggest splash, much to the giddy delight of my grandson and the much older lads too.

We strolled back down the hill to the café for a bacon sandwich. The conversation was allowed to develop according to John's financial insecurities and somehow ended up with him declaring that as an artist I have no idea what poverty is. I was actually offended by his remarks and was just about to tell him so, when Tony calmly diffused the situation by explaining that 'we've all experienced poverty in different ways at some point in our lives'. We all nodded in agreement, laughing at my grandson's face as he struggled with his fast melting ice-lolly.

End of diary extract no. 3

A walk in the hills was a suggestion from John and not something that Tony would normally fit into his spare time. I could sense that he was worried about the distance of the walk and the incline it involved but afterwards he was so proud that he had completed it given 'how unfit' he thought he was.

It was towards the end of the activity that it became clear that all members contribute to the facilitation process. Tony interjecting to diffuse a potential altercation between John and me is a good example of sharing the direction of the dialogue and a responsibility for the group.

Diary extract no. 4 – a reflection of the self

We had our usual breakfast meeting and talked for a few minutes about the wardrobes, which we had bought some weeks ago at a local antiques warehouse, not really sure what to use them for. Tony was in a bad mood due to lack of sleep and he seemed a bit cranky, and uninterested in the wardrobes. Instead, we made a list of words relating to caring, both negative and positive words, and he read the list out loud while I recorded it with the intention of playing it back inside the wardrobes as a mini art installation.

Negative words:

Sadness, resentment, guilt, helplessness, weak, detached, misinformed, scapegoated, invisible, soft, forsaken, downtrodden, misunderstood, forgotten, depressed, and unfocused.

Positive words:

Supportive, strong, caring, empathy, understanding, more rounded, mature, better informed, headstrong, focused, and happy.

End of diary extract no. 4

Part way through this very casual conversation, I became aware that we were painting a picture (in words) of Tony's life, an unseen part of him made visible for all to see, and also for him to see. That moment in the kitchen, presented us both with what the artist Stephen Willats refers to as 'the question', which enables participants to step back far enough to see an image of themselves and their own lives; a moment of detachment from the situation, and time enough to be critically objective, (Kester 2004).

Diary extract no. 5 – a change

I was expecting Tony to be down after England's football performance but he got in the car with a big smile on his face and went on to tell me how great he was feeling after not having a cigarette since Sunday. He'd also cut down his calorie intake and has been walking for about three miles per day; changing his food choices to include a healthier diet, less meat, less fat, and less sugar. We both spoke about how proud we were of him to take such a drastic life-changing step towards a positive future. He said he feels much better and is sleeping soundly too.

End of diary extract no. 5

No one had encouraged Tony to make the life-changing decisions that he'd made but they were important enough for him to share his joy at implementing the goals into his daily routine. As humans we are influenced by the company we keep and both Tony and I have managed to affect each other's lives. The behaviour and beliefs of one person influencing the other, arguably impacts on the development of local customs and cultures. For instance, I am a member of the local athletics club and have shared stories of running around the local hills for pleasure, and Tony's love for the local football club has influenced my decision to buy a season ticket. Could it be that our dialogical exchanges have led both of us to re-evaluate our lives and to make changes accordingly?

In Kester's model for a dialogical aesthetic he argues for an alternative approach to the way that art is interpreted and identifies a need to shift our understanding of the work of art towards the 'process of communicative exchange rather than a physical object', (Kester 2004, p. 90). With this in mind the intersubjective social exchanges between Tony and me reveal themselves as the work of art, which in turn locates itself deep in the everyday lives of participants.

Conclusion

> It is not by looking at things but by dwelling in them, that we understand their joint meaning (Polanyi & Sen 2009).

The activities that have occurred through Ingold's morphogenetic approach have produced periods of 'indwelling', offering each other an opportunity to see the world from another perspective. As Polanyi and Sen point out, it isn't enough to look at something in a bid to understand it, we must ultimately be able to empathise with the thing if we are ever to get close to understanding it, and seeing the thing in its own context is part of that process of understanding.

While Kester stipulates that 'we can never claim to fully inhabit the other's subject position' he adds that 'we can imagine, and this imagination, this approximation, can radically alter our sense of who we are' (Kester 2004 p. 115).

Kester's model for a dialogical aesthetic acknowledges the importance of listening and together with Polanyi and Sen's process of indwelling helps to contextualise the Men Who Care project in the here and now, with local truths '… recognising the social context from which others speak, judge and act' (Kester 2004, p. 113).

Ingold also identifies with this deep level of engagement as 'the artisan couples his own movements and gestures – indeed his very life – with the becoming of his materials, joining with and following the forces and flows that bring his work to fruition' (Ingold 2013, p. 31). He also recognises the need for space 'to allow knowledge to grow from the inside of being in the unfolding of life' (Ingold 2013, p. 8). The longevity of dialogical art projects depends on the sound foundations of sincere friendships and genuine interconnectedness, enhanced through the process of sharing real life experiences.

Bringing together the male carers on the canal barge at the beginning of the project presented the opportunity for tenuous links to grow into intimate bonds. None of us knew what would actually come out of that initial stranger-meets-stranger experience. No one foresaw the impact of the project on the health and well-being of the participants. Tony commented in the first few weeks how important it was for him to be able to chat to someone who doesn't verbally abuse him, putting him down for being on social benefits or for being overweight. His low self-esteem is something that I have witnessed a definite improvement in during the time we have spent together. From being unable to sit in the window at a fast food restaurant for fear of what people would think of him, to losing over three stones in weight and taking up regular exercise including walking and weight training. He is now calorie conscious and makes every effort to stick to his positive life-style changes.

We met almost every week for at least 2 hours for several months and every session involved dialogue. Sometimes we met with the intention of developing ideas about how to attract new members or suggestions for day trips, only to sit down in the kitchen with a brew and a catch-up on how their week had unfolded.

In the back of my mind, the artwork seemed to be developing in connection with a couple of wardrobes we'd bought one day while browsing a local auction house. We thought they would come in handy for storing things. I saw them for their functionality and felt that they somehow represented a forgotten kind of man. They looked very different on the outside (in size and design) but inside they were ordered just the same, with shelves labelled for specific items of a gentlemen's attire; socks, ties, shirts, collars, cufflinks etc. For many weeks they acted as an oversized larder for tea and coffee supplies as we sat discussing strategies to attract more members or pitching ideas for a creative activity programme. Those regular conversations became opportunities for participants to express concerns about their individual personal situations; each scenario quite different but connected deeply through the context of home caring, which is a subject I have no experience of. I listened as they shared their pain and frustration of being invisible, of not receiving the help they so desperately needed, of being trapped without proper social care and support.

I was gently moulded into the role of counsellor; the sessions becoming a sounding board for anything on their mind. I responded to the prodding and the shaping as I attempted to facilitate their frustrations caused by the lack of support from the government benefit system. I scoped out participant interests, trying to find common ground without getting into arguments, clashing of opinions or cultures. It would have been all too easy to hit a nerve or to say something offensive, given the low self-esteem of the group, due mainly to the lack of sleep on top of all the frustrations of being a carer in a world that appears not to care.

Hearing one participant telling another about how the regular meetings are a 'life-saver' is a great indication of how feedback is shared within and beyond the group, and it's not coerced from them, but instead they offer it, as a gift from the participants to the world around them. After a game of bowls with John and his friend, I overheard John telling his friend 'I know we don't do much at these Friday morning meetings but they are a real godsend and they keep me sane, I don't know what I would do without them'.

I've also witnessed changes in the behaviour of individual participants. I would often be asked technical advice regarding digital cameras and upon offering my advice the participant would change the subject, or ask another question before I had chance to finish the answer. More recently, and after many months of asking, the participant actually took it on board and started to use his camera in the session. This was a small but significant step for the participant. On another occasion, a participant and his wife told me that they can see a real positive change in his self-esteem due to the benefits of attending the regular meetings, which have led to improvements to his personal health and well-being; he himself claims he has grown in confidence enough to quit smoking, control a healthier diet, and to take up regular exercise.

As for the impact on the artist, I too had sleepless nights, often troubled by their harrowing stories, and sometimes just worrying about the sustainability of the group. My personal life was also affected in other ways due to the social proximity of participants. I live in the same borough and we know the same places, people, and shops and so on. We talked about old schools, local football clubs, favourite cafes and pubs, terrible transport networks, and old friends. The dialogical process produced moments of self-reflection, and in effect held up a mirror to all participants, including the artist. I've had my own moments of realisation about my personal life during the project and I've made changes, which are no doubt the results of being a participant in this project, from reconnecting with old school pals to buying season tickets to the local football club with my brother.

It was the Chilli-making house visit where I realised I was lacking some social skills, in respect of being a houseguest. It got me thinking about the last time I actually visited a friend, it was then that I realised I had lost contact with my closest friends. We can see from that particular diary entry that I'd had my own transformative moment in the project timeline.

Socially engaged art projects are heavily dependent on time to allow for things to happen naturally, with the artist and participants relying on what Ingold refers to as 'intuition in action' (Ingold 2013, p. 25). My projects do indeed evolve intuitively, they are live, emerging without rehearsal and no fixed design in mind, they work in and with the flow of life or as Ingold might say, with the grain of the wood (rather than against it). The artist's role as a facilitator of morphogenetic approaches brings with them a tacit understanding of the creative process and a confidence, which allows things to grow organically, in tune with the local environment, people and place.

Had I adopted a more hylomorphic method, with an end product in mind before I met the male carers group, then the social activities that we all took part in would arguably not have occurred: Crown Green Bowling, visits to art galleries, browsing antique shops, cooking at John's house, and walking in the local hills were all activities that emerged from open dialogue sessions with group. With a more hylomorphic approach, I would have steered the group towards developing and producing my vision, with little time for digression, and consequently little room for collective emergence to occur.

The hylomorphic approach identifies participants as tools and/or labour in the production of the artists' vision, while the morphogenetic approach allows for a shared creative vision to emerge through the process of intersubjective exchange. This morphogenetic understanding of creativity places the maker/artist in a more humble position than the one portrayed by the hylomorphic model where the artist as the 'genius' has a fixed predetermined design already in mind. The morphogenetic artist is a participant in the collective creative endeavours of shared experiences and this approach to engagement can be applied to Ingold's earthly materials and Kester's communities in the form of listening, responding, etc. There are clear crossovers and similarities within the context of the creativity processes at work. Ingold's mode of communication in the context of the maker responding to particular qualities of a given material like stone, wood or clay, and the inter-subjective encounters, of which Grant Kester refers to, work in a similar way; the artist engages in a series of interactions with potential participants/or materials.

There was a natural tension generated by the encounters and the social proximity of participants in this project. This tension was not dissimilar to Ingold's basket weaving exercise where the maker bends the willow branches into shape in order to create a weave: 'The form was not imposed on the material from without, but rather generated in this force field, comprised by the relations between the weaver and the willow' (Ingold 2013, p. 22). Similarly, it is the direct social connection between each other, which provides the necessary tension/friction between all the participants, holding the network together and attributing to its overall dynamic. The regular inter-subjective exchanges between participants are crucial properties of the network, enabling it to develop, expanding or contracting, and ultimately contributing to the potential of an emerging collective future. Tension often revealed itself in communications, whether engaging in small talk, planning a shared experience or non-participation in group activities. It all depended how life was treating each participant at that particular moment in time.

In the same way that exploring the physical qualities of a certain material strengthens the relationship between the material and the maker, leading to unexpected forms, conversations can often lead into unknown territories and it takes a lot of trust and confidence on both sides to allow that to happen in a way that produces positive results. Grant Kester refers to a 'discursive space' (p. 122), where artists and participants are not bound by a fixed topical agenda but allowed to digress in conversation, ultimately progressing through dialogue towards some kind of personal transformation in the form of new perspectives and insights.

Even though the commission has ended I'm still 'in residence' in another way. I can't simply walk away, I'm already deeply rooted in the area, having been born and bred there, the project has been started but an end has not yet been designated.

As Tim Ingold points out, making is very much a social activity between the maker and the materials, a communication of tension between both forces. When the artist is a participant among participants in the creative process, embedded socially engaged art practice is located at the morphogenetic end of the spectrum. In the context of the male carers group, the inter-subjective exchanges between all the participants (including the artist) occur on a deeply intimate and personal level. It is a level where at times the blurring of everyday life and art go unnoticed and sometimes the art of participation is stretched to the point of breaking down but always … things happen and shared meanings emerge.

References

Ingold, T. (2013). *Making: Anthropology, archeology, art and architecture*. London: Routledge.

Kester, G. H. (2004). *Conversation Pieces: Community and communication in modern art*. Berkeley: University of California Press.

Polanyi, M., & Sen, A. (2009). *The tacit dimension*. Chicago: The University of Chicago Press.

Web sites

Creative people and places (CCP). 2017. Retrieved from http://www.creativepeopleplaces.org.uk

TITLEY - CROCIANI-WINDLAND

The act of creation for Titley is a similar or even the same process as the process of relational engagement. Boundaries are blurred. The male carers create, the artist cares. They are all careful and caring and creating together. Unspoken dilemmas can relocate into new spaces that lead to Deleuzian 'becomings', intensities of affect, of invisible lives becoming-visible. This life made visible and validated through a recognition of its actual experienced existence connects us to Lita Crociani-Windland's piece Deleuze, art and social work. Through the process of making, the maker becomes the material, becomes the patterns of an artwork, as Crociani-Windland demonstrates through her own personal experience: the nervous system becomes the twists of the crochet work; the tension is turned into material. Through a Deleuzian ontological approach to the potential of making art to redefine what it means to celebrate process and experience, Crociani-Windland expresses a desire for a social work practice that tends towards a celebration of creativity that makes a life one of hope for the future rather than depressed by any past trajectory. Social work viewed in this way and experienced as such can be transformed from problem solving to ways of living creatively with others, a celebration of difference instead of sameness. The importance of the artwork is not in the outcome-object but in the experience and intensity of the sensation it imbues or transmits; similarly, Crociani-Windland urges us to consider that social work should aspire to and mirror the process of creation. It is art and the making and experiencing of art that can teach us to be positive with uncertainty. From this Deleuzian perspective 'solutions' are not solutions; process is all; artworks are sensation and intensities. Through the arts and crafts, a process of what Crociani-Windland calls 'foregrounding' and 'backgrounding' is activated and becomes a process of difference in repetition. Each creative act — for example the weaving of a thread — becomes a repeated act which is nevertheless different to the previous one. Through the relationship between the creator and the created, the affective connections that form the tapestry of a person's life can be mirrored in the artistic act of creation. Through the intensities of this act of creation an indirect route to personal and relational affect is created from the Deleuzian 'virtual' which is invisible and unspoken to something more visible while still unspoken. This, then is another way of engaging in a living process, in acceptance of the difficult invisible that can be positively encountered and re-assessed in and for the benefit of social work practice.

Lita Crociani-Windland

DELEUZE, ART AND SOCIAL WORK

This article outlines the value of Deleuze's philosophy to social work in offering a different understanding of the constitution of reality and being human and the importance of the visual by way of artistic and craft activities. The key concepts derived from Deleuze's work and outlined in the article concern the idea of the 'virtual' as relevant to the concept of 'a life' and 'difference and repetition' as a way of conceptualising an anti-essentialist post-modern view of identity as fragmented, but dynamic. In other words partaking of chaotic, but also creative potential. This conceptualisation of life allows to think about all lives, even 'difficult' ones, as potentially creatively undetermined in the future, rather than just pathologically predetermined by the past. Arts and crafts are seen as having the power to provoke and soothe, allowing a process of discovery of what the material and the person might both become in the doing. Thus, the article offers an ontological grounding validating arts and crafts, experiential learning and apprenticeship models as essential to social work practice and training at a time when these might be driven out by evidence-based paradigms and budget cuts.

Introduction

The argument put forward in this article is that Deleuze's philosophy offers a way of understanding how visual imagination as part of art and craft activities opens possibilities for reframing one's experiences and working with problems. In order to validate and explicate this claim it introduces some of Deleuze's key ideas to offer a particular ontological and epistemological grounding for the importance of visual arts and crafts in the practice of social work. This is important in the light of evidence-based and scientific/positivistic models having restricted what is valued and given time, in a period of unprecedented cuts to social care budgets.

For those unfamiliar with the terms ontology and epistemology, ontology refers to the 'nature of being', or to put it another way what we believe the nature of reality to be, while epistemology concerns the study and practices that might arise from what we believe that nature of being and reality to be. Deleuze's philosophical framework offers a very different, often very abstract way of thinking about the nature of being and of reality, more concerned with understanding change and process, than with outcomes. Simply put, process is about how one lives in the world, how one is affected by one's context and surroundings and how one affects them, in other words it is about the more fluid aspects of life, mostly happening below the level of consciousness.

While there is literature about the value of arts and crafts in the field of Social Work (see most recently in the *British Journal of Social Work* Moxley & Feen 2015; Trevelyan, Crath, & Chambon 2014; Tudor, Maidment, Campbell, & Whittaker 2015), my aim here is to outline what the philosophy of Deleuze offers to an understanding of why arts and crafts need to be valued in both the practice and the training of social workers. It is noted by many authors (Bell 2012, gives an excellent overview) that ontological issues have been relatively neglected and that this gap creates inconsistency between ontological foundations, epistemology, ethical aims of the profession and mainstream practice. This article therefore aims to make a small contribution to this needed development of 'post-conventional' (Bell 2012) ontological and theoretical grounding in the field.

To do this, the article starts with a Deleuzian view on the nature of being human, which is then followed by a reflexive narrative to explicate, ground and exemplify what follows from such ontological tenets. As often those entrusted to the social care profession are those suffering what Goffman (2009) would term 'spoiled identity', identity, seen as dynamic and embodied, open to contradictions and disorder (Deleuze 2004 2005; Deleuze & Guattari 1999), is the starting point. This allows the introduction of how difference and repetition are conceptualised as key to it in Deleuze's (2004) work. These concepts are also later related to artistic practices and are embedded in a wider understanding of life as composed of a duality. This duality is not one of nature and culture or mind and body, rather Deleuze (following Bergson) proposes that alongside what is actualised in our embodied, historical existence another realm is continuously present, while being out of sight. The term used to denote this less visible, beneath the surface, but real domain is the 'virtual' (not to be confused with virtual as in virtual reality). This formulation acknowledges mostly unseen forces and tensions in our lives that lead to actual events, but by doing so restricts the potential, that all of us have, to respond to them creatively. The argument being developed is that arts and crafts give access to that realm and its potential, by freeing up imagination, while giving expression to the tensions and conflicts underlying actual problems, creating the opportunity to change our relation to them and move forward in a new way. Arts and craft activities have the capacity to provoke and soothe, to open up a process of discovery of what the material and the person might both become in the doing.

This framework offers an alternative perspective to the dominant neo-liberal, evidence-based and medicalised discourses. While the value of art is not a new idea, a positivist and reductive paradigm allied to neo-liberal policies has meant that this aspect of practice, when and if it happens, is most often unsupported by institutional structures (Moxley & Feen 2015).

Identity, difference and repetition and a bit of contextual framing in relation to social work

The word identity gives us a clue to what is normally regarded as key to it, namely being 'idem' –Latin for same – over time. In Deleuze's and much post-modern theory no such thing is possible in a literal sense and most of us can acknowledge in a commonsense way that who I am now cannot be quite the same as who I was many years ago, yet most of us have a sense of continuity under normal circumstances. Our bodies give an example of that: they are continually changing; cell renewal means that in reality our bodies are never the same. The paradox is that in spite of this, we are recognisable to ourselves and others, unless some majorly traumatic event occurs or we choose to change our appearance in major ways. Difference and repetition, as Deleuze (2004) points out, are not oppositional binaries, but relationally implicated with each other: for things to stay the same, continuous renewal is required. Our bodies as well as our identity over time rely on this relation between difference and repetition for the experience of continuity. In Deleuze's (2004) view, repetition always involves difference, it is never repetition of the same. What we repeat is the overall pattern of relations that make us who we are, while the elements that are in relation are always in flux. Art follows the same process: we use different materials to express our perceptions and experiences. The artistic production is not the object, just as the map is not the territory, but a different re-presentation (used in the sense of presenting anew) of our encounter with it through a different medium. This I hope will become clearer as I expand on the theoretical frame with examples in the following sections of the article.

While the continuous process of change, both inner and outer, ensures our survival, it is the aspect we are least aware of. We tend to take it for granted, prizing the sameness that it is seemingly in service to. There is a hierarchical ordering here and an oppositional stance. The sameness (*you don't look a day older!*) is seen as an aspect of health, while pathologising has its field day in its disruptions, making use of the relative ubiquity of some aspects of change and development by normalising them, while highlighting others as anomalies to be got rid of, more often than understood. This is where people with dementia, intellectual disabilities and/or traumatised and/or disordered lives show us aspects of being human with a problematic social and policy history. We have moved away from the more severe manifestations of not wanting to see them or be reminded of them, by no longer locking people up in segregated institutions. Yet having attempted to rectify the situation through care in the community and other policies, other new and different problems have taken the place of old ones. In extreme cases the learning disabled or mentally unwell requiring acute intervention are often wrongfully placed in secure institutions or prisons that have replaced the old institutions (segregated residential/ asylums). Dealing with less extreme difference, on the other hand, relies on over-optimistic faith in the capacities of individuals, families and (fast disintegrating) communities to care in an often culturally and materially impoverished environment. Thus, social and other care work these days is not only having to be outcome and bio-medically driven, but fragmented and often reduced to the provision of statutory duties. Bell (2012) and others argue that the inconsistency between social work's modernist ontological foundations and many of social work's epistemological concepts, such as anti-oppressive and critical approaches, represents a major contradiction in the conceptualisation of the profession's philosophical base. New approaches are needed.

Adopting a Deleuzian view, identity is about a dynamic relation between difference and sameness, open to change and 'becoming' and encompassing disordered states of mind as part of everyone's make-up. These are seen as potentially creative, rather than just dysfunctional. This allows it to chime with the ethical concerns of social justice, notions of equality and non-discriminatory practices that have animated the profession. Art and craft allow for that creativity to be accessed. I have mentioned a particular kind of duality at the heart of Deleuze's philosophy. This is expressed in synthesis in Deleuze's last essay *A Life* (2005).

'A life'

The Deleuzian concept of '*a* life' can be understood as equivalent to the 'virtual' in relation to an individual. 'A life' is unique, 'impersonal and yet singular' (Deleuze, 2005, pp. 8–9). It does not require a conscious process of individualisation and can never be completely specified. It is something that underlies '*the* life' of the individual, it is the hidden, though real realm of forces and tensions that give rise to 'their' life. It is 'pure immanence', that is something underlying, deeply implicated in all of reality (Williams in Parr, 2005, pp. 125–127), generative of, yet not superior too, actual conditions of existence. It is something we might be able to connect to more closely in significant moments of intensity.

> *A* life is everywhere, in all the moments that a given living subject goes through and that are measured by given living objects: an immanent life carrying with it the events and singularities that are merely actualized in subjects and objects. [...] The singularities and the events that constitute *a* life coexist with the accidents of *the* life that corresponds to it, but they are neither grouped nor divided in the same way (Deleuze, 2005, pp. 29–30).

His essay *Immanence: A Life* from which the above quote is derived is his last piece of writing, some would call it a sort of testament (Deleuze 2005, p. 20); short and hard to decipher without prior exposure to his work, it gives us a final synthesis of what his work tries to open up for us: a different way of thinking about the world, that encompasses both the material and actual world we live in and its real, but not actualised, generative conditions. Let me give you an example: a complex combination of push/pull factors is usually involved in migration, these factors range from environmental, personal as well as political. When the tensions of existence in one's place of origin or residence become too intense, the result is migration. That is the actual event, but those tensions have generated it and only some aspects may be readily identified. Others remain beneath the surface unknown to the migrant like me (I was born and grew up in Italy): I only became fully aware of a trajectory initiated three generations back through an ethnographic journey back to my Italian roots. The conditions for my coming to England were far more complex than I had known till then. My life is here in England; 'a life' includes all the influences I absorbed in Italy and still link me to that place. The general realm of these conditions is what is meant by the 'virtual': a transcendental realm of interconnections, tensions and relations of forces, encompassing all of existence: it is where the potentiality of the world resides, its variety and indeterminacy, which is continuously transformed into our actual living. As such, it encompasses the natural and environmental forces that underlie the world we live in, as well as the unconscious processes of the human mind.

'A life', rather than 'the life of' or 'my life' or 'my identity' indicates both a generality and a specificity, which is not about possession, as in 'my life', or judgement (Deleuze 2005). We cannot refrain from judgement about having a good or a bad life, we are so used to it. Our judgements are often superficial and based on repertoires of categories, which those less familiar with them would neither necessarily agree with nor recognise themselves within. The idea of 'poverty', for example, is not something non-modern societies would recognise about themselves, it is an etic concept, i.e. a concept belonging to outsiders to that context. Take the idea of victimhood and dependency. Why does benefit fraud so enrage public opinion? Of course there is more than one answer (see Crociani-Windland and Hoggett (2012) for a different one), but given its very low incidence (.9%) and low impact in the grand scheme of things, what may be one of its most effective powers to offend is that it puts two fingers up to the idea of the dispossessed as poor victims. It turns the tables on the accustomed, 'proper' order of things; it transgresses the emotional economy of power. Choosing a life on the streets is something few 'housed minds' can appreciate as a choice. It is rather conceived as a matter of personal irresponsibility, rather than a reasonable response to conditions that make it the best one might be able to aspire to at a particular time or on a more permanent basis (see Scanlon & Adlam 2006). The possibility that such choice may be actually about a life that has kept closer to chaos and indeterminacy in a positive way and learned to live with problems as best it can, does not often get taken seriously. Yet this is what Deleuze would advocate: the art and craft of living with problems, rather than the resolution or elimination of them. This does not of course mean we should just stop thinking about the conditions that have made that the best option for some, though it takes us away from stigmatising and thinking of such situations in a reductive and individualised way.

It also offers hope, something much needed in any work that involves exposure to people in distress and in need of care. It offers a positive view: 'a life' is always in the making (Scanlon & Adlam 2006, pp. 13–14). This is true for all of us and all of us partake of moments or events that lead us to disordered states, what Deleuze would term 'pre-subjective delirium' and 'pre-individual singularity'. These terms are used to denote a zone or plane of indeterminacy in any person's make up. These terms are suggestive of the chaotic, the personality disordered, the discontinuous or irrational. This is often what disenfranchised, autistic, mentally unstable persons and, according to Deleuze, children show us: they are singular, we could not confuse them with someone else, yet they are not necessarily coherent and self-aware. Often they are more capable of intensity and passion, than supposedly better adjusted, more ordered characters. Could this be an indication of a closer relation to 'a life', to the 'virtual', rather than 'my life'?

The idea of 'a life' is about immanence, process, virtuality (Deleuze 2005, pp. 28–31) and in turn these are to do with potentiality, to a being open to becomings and transformations (Deleuze & Guattari 1999). The idea of care and social work are transformed by this perspective from an elimination of, or dealing with, problems to a relational stance that is about how to live with (and help others to live with) problems in as creative a way as possible. Art has a place in this; as Rajchman puts it: "Deleuze came to think that artworks just *are* sensations connected in materials ... Through affect and percept artworks hit upon something singular yet impersonal in our bodies and brains, irreducible to any pre-existent 'we'" (Deleuze 2005, pp. 9–10). In this case the pre-existent 'we' should be understood as referring to an essentialist notion of identity, which Deleuze does not subscribe to. Art is not primarily about thought or judgement, but sensation based experience.

Lives, affect, art and the potential for the new

Virtuality as the indeterminate (yet determining) (back)ground of reality has a correlate in the notion of affect. Deleuze and Guattari (1999, p. xvi) see affect as "a prepersonal intensity corresponding to the passage from one experiential state of the body to another". As such that passage is marked by sensation, yet the sensation is not determined a priori, but is open to qualification (Massumi 2002). Qualification is the process by which we interpret some experience as pleasant or unpleasant or anything more subtly in between, and this interpretation is dependent on/is in relation to a host of other experiences that may be part of our individual present and past actual life. That actual life however does partake of the potential of the new, by being also always connected to the pre-personal and virtual plane. This means all lives, even 'difficult' ones are potentially creatively undetermined in the future, rather than just pathologically predetermined by the past. This shifts the focus and gives a priority to affective encounters and to affective conditions that include environmental aspects.

This links to a different understanding of health and freedom, as Duff (2014, p. 19) notes in Deleuzian terms: "health is advanced or promoted in the provision of new affective sensitivities and new relational capacities".

> Health may, indeed, be characterised in more Deleuzian terms as a differential process of becoming reasonable, strong and free, where freedom is understood not in some totalising way synonymous with a prevailing moral order, but rather as a specific moment of rupture or transformation in which something new emerges in an active expression of creativity and invention (Duff 2014, p. 17).

The role of creative practices such as art and craft activities is that they might afford the opportunity to reconfigure our affective connections and qualifications. They allow the foregrounding of some aspects of one's experience, while putting others in the background, affecting therefore perception and its qualifications, with all the ramifications that might activate. This relation and interplay between foregrounding and backgrounding is what is also involved in art (Deleuze 2004, p. 31).

In Deleuzian terms "the arts produce and generate intensity, that which directly impacts the nervous system and intensifies sensation" (Grosz 2008, p. 3). This is what in my view gives them the power to reshape processes of engagement with the world. The arts in this conceptualisation are not about the production of concepts, rather they produce affects and intensities able to address problems and provocations (Grosz 2008, p. 1). While conceptualising is not their aim, they may give rise to different affects and intensities that may align or link to different ways of thinking about problems. While artistic practices are not aimed at solving problems, they may give rise to ways of living with them in terms of changing one's relation to them.

Art, experience, expertise and apprenticeship

In Deleuze's philosophy process is key. Process, in very simplistic terms, is about how something happens; how one lives in the world, how one is affected by one's context and surroundings and how one affects them, in other words it is about movements, speeds, relationality, mostly happening below the level of consciousness. Deleuze and Guattari (1999) talk about a molecular level of becoming and transformation, happening at a subtle and mostly unconscious level: "... 'learning' always takes place in and through the unconscious, thereby establishing the bond of a profound complicity between nature and mind" (Deleuze 2004, p. 205). Affective expressions – a smile, a gesture, a greeting, a way of holding – may be more important than what we know, say or do. While knowledge is needed, it is not sufficient in itself: expertise needs an experiential and relational dimension, which is of enormous therapeutic value. The word 'expertise' shares an etymological root with experience and experiential, after all, and what is meant by experience is not about what is known in academic terms, but what is learnt from practice. Some things cannot easily be learnt from books, but need to be learnt by doing. This is where the notion of apprenticeship is important. For instance, it is one thing to know about challenging behaviour in theory, another to encounter it, be affected by it and learn to regulate our own affective response, the fear, frustration, anger or confusion and learn from it. The external challenge and our own response mark a profound encounter that involves both parties in an intense relationship with external and internal experiences. It can bring deep learning not just about the other, but also ourselves, if deeply engaged with in both directions. Emphasising this aspect in social work, education and care training more generally and not just in relation to this more extreme example would in my view be extremely useful, as would the provision of practice supervision.

To return to Deleuze's philosophy and art – Sauvagnargues (2013) argues that he has created a semiotic of creativity, based on an experiential rather than phenomenological approach (Aroles & McLean 2016) and most of his work deals with art of all kinds (Grosz 2008; Sauvagnargues 2013). Arts and crafts involve a relation with materials, they rely on the senses, yet connect also to what is beyond the senses. To illustrate the relation of body, materials and the forces and relations beyond the senses, Deleuze (2004, pp. 204–205) gives the example of how to think of the sea (drawing from Leibniz) and learning to swim. The difficulty of the passage that follows may show how much easier it is to learn to swim than to theorise it and may also illustrate the challenge I have in trying to communicate what is a dense, but extremely useful set of ideas. Deleuze speaks of the sea and the 'idea' of the sea as a system of differential relations, the totality of which is expressed in the real movement of the waves, and learning to swim as the conjugation

> of the distinctive points of our bodies with the singular points of the objective Idea in order to form a problematic field. This conjugation determines for us a threshold of consciousness at which our real acts are adjusted to our perceptions of the real relations, thereby providing a solution to the problem (Deleuze 2004, pp. 204–205).

While not everyone can swim, it is harder to explain in words and to unpack theoretically, than it is to learn from practice. For a very humorous rendition of the limitations of an intellectual only approach to learning I recommend reading Alexander McCall-Smith's (2004) *The Two and a Half Pillars of Wisdom*, where academics attempt to learn to play tennis and to swim from a book, with hilarious and ultimately tragic results.

The experiential aspect is key to Deleuze's notion of apprenticeship of living with problems (Deleuze 2004, pp. 204–205). In the past much vocational training was delivered through apprenticeships: in the UK this only dwindled around 1900 (Lane 1996) and there is a current move towards re-establishing them as part of Higher Education programmes (Skills Funding Agency 2015). Medieval apprentices would live with and learn their trade from a master craftsman, apprenticeships could last from seven to 14 years. Most Medieval and Renaissance painters had their schools and apprentices often painted large parts of a canvas; Medieval Craft Guilds passed on their expertise this way. This is because organising the materials, learning to use them and creating some expression is a complex process best learnt through a physical engagement and the role modelling of someone who has mastered the encounter with the materials. That encounter sets us against not only the resistance of the materials themselves, what they can and will do and what they will not, and connects us to our own bodies, but also confronts us with our limitations, resistance and preconceptions. I have experienced first-hand the power of such activities to provoke and soothe. I do not consider myself an artist, but I dabble, I use art and crafts as therapeutic tools for myself and have even taught art for a period of my life. I was fortunate to have an artistic mother and grandparents skilled in different crafts, all practical people able to make things. I learnt to embroider when very young; I can crochet, knit, sew and have the basics of spinning and weaving. I started to crochet again recently to relieve stress and found myself having the sense that what I was actually doing was transferring the tension and twistedness of my nervous system into the twists of the crochet: as I hooked, turned and twisted the yarn, I felt my tension flow out of me and transform into a piece of usable material; my stress became productive and dissolved, at least for a while. Adult colouring books have become popular and advocated by mindfulness practitioners as a way to 'distract' service users away from stress or distress, but another way of thinking about this is to see their potential as bringing repetition to bear on difference, in other words bringing order to chaos (I understand this to be the value of my Sudoku playing habit before going to sleep and possibly the source of its popularity). On the other hand I have also tried to paint the skies I have so enjoyed observing after a recent house move and have been totally infuriated by my incapacity and lack of skill. To put it in Deleuzian terms, I cannot (yet) conjugate the 'Idea' of the clouds, the interplay of light, air and water, with my handling of the paint medium. I could use a period of apprenticeship to learn this.

Having said this, one must add that knowing how to use the materials is part of the discovery and making a painting one is satisfied with is also part of the pleasure. What is involved is a disciplined experiential approach of learning what you can do with what and how to do it, which can sometimes result in more than one expected. As Grosz (2008, p. 4) puts it: "Art enables matter to become expressive, to not just satisfy, but also to intensify – to resonate and become more than itself". To return briefly to 'difference and repetition', one of the ways we can see art's endeavour is as the expression of the differential relations of whatever we wish to present anew (rather than represent) by using different materials. It is about a visual imagination (re)producing those relations through materials other than those of the original event or natural manifestation, involving difference for the (re)creation of the same.

I know several people for whom art is a profoundly terrifying activity; it can feel humiliating and shaming. Mostly this has to do with dashed expectations of control and mastery, preconceived ideas and ambitions, bad school experiences and the sense of regression that adults can experience in trying to do something held in high social status and commercially valued on the one hand (museums and art galleries being high culture) and childish play on the other. This is a particularly big problem when we try to create art. The crafts are less problematic by being given a lower social status to art, by being less idealised and more practically oriented towards producing useful items. Yet both arts and crafts partake of an encounter with what Benjamin (2004) might term the lawfulness of materials, meaning what can and cannot be done with them, and both involve the organising and practice of processes, both technical and in excess of what is needed for pure survival. Choosing one's tools needs to relate to both task and material. Going against the grain of the wood will not produce enjoyment or a good result. The making of a knitted jumper is never just about warmth, but also includes design and creativity of some kind. Chairs come in all sorts of different designs, shapes and details telling us so much about those who made them, when and for what purpose as well as telling us about those whose chairs they might be or become. Marx made it the key to his idea of what makes us different from animals, though a Deleuzian view would contest this as a unique human capacity (see Grosz 2008).

The provocativeness of arts and crafts, the challenges they pose to us through the particular qualities of different materials, is aggravated by our tendency to focus on outcomes, rather than on a process of discovery of what the material and the person might both become in the doing. My experience of teaching painting to learning disabled young people was that there was relatively little resistance, the 'self' was getting less in the way of the activity. This I believe to be a useful initial approach for people at any stage of life: to approach art as play and experimentation and offer it as such to begin with. This is not to be understood again in a hierarchically structured and judgemental way that might see it as an invitation to regression, itself a term charged with negative connotations. Rather, it should be seen as a move to the source and foundation of our social and cultural life as Winnicott pointed out (1971) and in Deleuzian terms as a 'becoming-child' (Deleuze & Guattari 1999). This is the process of finding the receptivity, youthfulness and vitality of each stage of life, not at all a regressive notion. Rather it is a notion deeply linked to development at all ages, congruent with the earlier statement that "health is advanced or promoted in the provision of new affective sensitivities and new relational capacities". The links made between a dynamic notion of identity, open to transformation in the future and the role of art in offering the possibility for such transformation, reframing and reimagining one's life, offer a different ontological base to the modernist prevailing view which entails a refocusing on process and affective encounters in promoting health.

Conclusion

A Deleuzian approach to care and social work means a promotion of non-pathologising, non-judgemental attitudes and an emphasis on affective dimensions of practice, including art and craft activities, rather than outcome-oriented practices. While this may already be part of what social workers do and art may have been far more important to practice in the past (England 1986), the focus on performance and outcomes prevalent in neo-liberal management practices may be relegating this to the common sense and ethical orientation of individual practitioners. This should instead be regarded as a keystone of training and practice with ontological and epistemological foundations able to fully promote the importance of artistic and craft practices as part of what might offer opportunities for creative transformation (Parr 2005, pp. 57–59), something that for Deleuze and Guattari (1999) is both experiential and social (Parr 2005: 59). The fact that this way of thinking includes environmental, social and psychological aspects in a complex interrelation allows us to think in terms of enabling environments that will also include physical settings and arrangements, social interactions and other aspects key to affective impact.

However my focus for present purposes has been on offering the foundation for a non-judgemental relationality based on a particular understanding of our common humanity in that all of us may experience times of 'pre-personal subjectivity', disorientation, contradictions and less than well integrated identities in both personal and professional lives. We all share this aspect of the human condition, if we accept this framework it is an ontological ground. Whether we can withstand that experience and are able to use it creatively is what matters. This does not mean we do not need knowledge and professional expertise, but that relationality, affective encounters really matter and have to be part of that expertise. It gives us a better place to start from in relating to others, a place that may acknowledge differences and give us a way of acknowledging and relating to aspects of humanity we have in common that may be less than coherent or seemingly irrational. It might make us less afraid of our own vulnerabilities, which in turn might allow us to more open to learning, which involves experience (and mistakes). It may foster compassion, not in a condescending gesture towards the less fortunate, but in terms of its etymological roots: to suffer with, to share in a human condition, rather than feel somehow above it and professionally detached, while acknowledging the strain this might put on us and how sometimes we can't but defend ourselves by detaching or be in danger of becoming too identified.

Thinking this way means that by being always connected to the pre-personal, to 'a life', actual life also always partakes of the potential of the new. This opens us to seeing even 'difficult' lives as potentially creatively undetermined in the future, rather than just pathologically predetermined by the past. Art in this conceptualisation produces affects and intensities able to connect to 'a life', to that indeterminate aspect of our existence (Grosz 2008, p. 1). How we relate to the intensity and affective singularities of others matters. Art and craft can produce encounters with that intensity, may enable both parties to work with resistances, contradictions and elicit communication, by giving indirect ways of expressing that which is hard to talk about.

To conclude: the potential of creative practices is to give expression to problems and provocations and potentially help to reconfigure our affective connections, foregrounding some aspects of experience, while putting others in the background. This means that how we relate to those experiences, how good or bad or how important we might judge them to be may change. That change may in turn give us new possibilities. While artistic practices are not aimed at solving problems, in that this way of thinking acknowledges life itself as problematic by its very nature, they may give rise to ways of living with them. This way of thinking gives room for hope in the future, something needed by both professionals and those entrusted to their care in difficult and uncertain times.

References

Aroles, J., & McLean, C. (2016). Deciphering signs: An empirical apprenticeship. *Ethnography*, 1–18.

Bell, K. (2012). Towards a post-conventional philosophical base for social work. *British Journal of Social Work, 42*, 408–423.

Benjamin, J. (2004). Beyond doer and done to: An intersubjective view of thirdness. *Psychoanalytic Quarterly, LXXIII*, 5–46.

Crociani-Windland, L., & Hoggett, P. (2012). Politics and affect. *Subjectivity, 5*, 161–179.

Deleuze, G. (2004). *Difference and repetition*. London: The Athlone Press.

Deleuze, G. (2005). *Pure immanence-essays on a life*. New York, NY: Zone Books.

Deleuze, G., & Guattari, F. (1999). *A thousand plateaus*. London: The Athlone Press.

Duff, C. (2014). *Assemblages of health*. Dordrecht: Springer.

England, H. (1986). *Social work as art: Making sense for good practice*. London: Allen and Unwin.

Goffman, I. (2009). *Stigma: Notes on the management of spoiled identity*. London: Simon and Schuster.

Gray, M., & Webb, S. (2008). Social work as art revisited. *International Journal of Social Welfare, 17*, 182–193. doi:10.1111/j.1468-2397.2008.00548.x

Grosz, E. (2008). *Chaos, territory, art – Deleuze and the framing of the earth*. New York, NY: Columbia University Press.

Lane, J. (1996). *Apprenticeship in England, 1600–1914*. London: UCL Press.

Massumi, B. (2002). *Parables for the virtual: Movement, affect, sensation*. Durham, NC: Duke University Press.

McCall-Smith, A. (2004). *The two and a half pillars of wisdom*. Ilford: Abacus.

Moxley, D., & Feen, H. (2015). Arts-inspired design in the development of helping interventions in social work: Implications for the integration of research and practice. *British Journal of Social Work, 46*, 1690–1707. doi:https://doi.org/10.1093/bjsw/bcv087

Parr, A. (2005). *The Deleuze dictionary*. Edinburgh: Edinburgh University Press.

Sauvagnargues, A. (2013). *Deleuze and art*. (A. Bankston, Trans.). London: Bloomsbury.

Scanlon, C., & Adlam, J. (2006). Housing 'unhoused minds': Inter-personality disorder in the organisation? *Housing, Care and Support, 9*, 9–14. Retrieved September 29, 2016, from doi: 10.1108/14608790200600018

Skills Funding Agency. (2015). *Higher and degree apprenticeships – Information for employers and HEIs*. Retrieved December 9, 2016, from https://www.gov.uk/government/collections/sfa-higher-and-degree-apprenticeships

Trevelyan, C., Crath, R., & Chambon, A. (2014). Promoting critical reflexivity through arts-based media: A case study. *British Journal of Social Work, 44*, 7–26. doi:10.1093/bjsw/bcs090

Tudor, R., Maidment, J., Campbell, A., & Whittaker, K. (2015). Examining the role of craft in post-earthquake recovery: Implications for social work practice. *British Journal of Social Work, 45*(suppl 1), i205–i220. doi:10.1093/bjsw/bcv126

Winnicott, D. W. (1971). *Playing and reality*. London: Routledge.

Crociani-Windland - Trustram

Following on from Crociani-Windland's consideration of the relevance and use of arts and crafts in the lives of vulnerable people Myna Trustram draws our attention, once more to the setting of the museum as an arena for observation and reflection that can inform social work practice. Although she begins her article by voicing a nervousness in venturing into and commenting on the world of social work, social work practitioners and academics will find much of value and resonance with what she writes as she considers how suffering can act as a spur to art. The space and distance necessary in order for a work of art to be arranged and contemplated might allow for the emergence of enhanced empathic understanding that could not be achieved without occupying this space.

Trustram draws attention to the value of the museum as a place in which civilizations can show what they value and preserve what is left and, in doing so, she echoes Freud's contention that archaeology has a special place in the history of psychoanalysis. She questions whether museums can help us to "see what we see" so that we can see beyond what restricts and is perceivable, through to that which could and might be. The experience of a powerful arrangement of exhibits in a museum can help the viewer feel 'less alone'. This is a valuable and essential aspiration of effective social work practice and one which permeates several contributions throughout this special edition. By showing the pain of others the gallery simultaneously bears, preserves and 'provides a bulwark against' this pain.

While illustrating the function and value of the museum gallery Trustram shows how a dream she dreamt has relevance to her work. There is also a thought-provoking discussion of exhibits that encourage the viewer to (literally) "take something away" as well as bring something to what is shown. The changing nature of the exhibit in the process of being viewed recalls the melting ice sculpture described by Malone in a previous article in this journal. Works of art including an older woman living alone in a tower block, a sapling held by a post, study for a sudden gust of wind, institutional bunk beds and travellers caught in a sudden breeze, are all discussed. The status of works not exhibited, "wrapped up within their own melancholy, waiting for some future", are considered as is "the night time security" that is put in place to protect exhibits. Towards the end of the article Trustram writes, "The space and pace are here every day and can be used, or not". Although written by someone not currently practising as a social worker, what the author conveys has much to offer to and inform social work thinking, practice and writing. We urge you to enjoy the space provided here at your own pace and to see what emerges from it.

Myna Trustram

ACCOUNTING FOR THE MUSEUM

In this essay for the Journal of Social Work Practice I bring the practices of writing, reading, visiting, imagining and above all looking, to the forefront of a critical enquiry into museums. It's part of a wider endeavour to use critical and creative writing to account for museums and to clear space for a different kind of writing. I am drawing together some reading and visits to art museums that I made in the summer of 2016, in order to think about the relevance that the work of museums might have for social work. I endeavoured to be in the museums and in the reading with a freely associative mind and imagination. The essay enacts the form of my fragmentary thinking whilst I was doing this.

§ I am nervous of venturing into this world of social work. Ostensibly because to spend your days looking at art seems incomparable to how I imagine a social worker spends her days. And whilst of course there's plenty of suffering in art and pleasure in social work, perhaps the worlds coalesce around this question of the visual imagination. A rough sleeper on the street is both a representation of suffering, a spur to the imagination, and a real sufferer; as is, say, a self-portrait by Frida Kahlo, they are compelling because they are both real and imagined. But I still feel a need for museums, and those who work in them, to account for themselves. Not because there is a clamouring for this to be done or to indulge a sense of professional unworthiness, more to find some ease from the demands of conscience; especially if that conscience has been formed in thrall to Christian liturgy, as has mine. For this reason I'm drawn to Judith Butler's *Giving an Account of Oneself* (2005), for the attention it brings to the idea of accountability. There's been a lot of accounting for museums within the academic discipline of Museum Studies, a lot of arguments for their social efficacy, but little that employs a psychodynamic understanding.

§ The philosopher Judith Butler ends a short unpublished lecture called 'Speaking of Rage and Grief' with these words,

> With great speed we do sometimes drive away from the unbearable, or drive precisely into its clutches, or do both at once, not knowing how we move or with what consequence. It seems unbearable to be patient with unbearable loss, and yet that slowness, that impediment can be the condition for *showing what we value,* and even perhaps what steps to take to *preserve what is left* of what we love (Butler 2014, my italics).

She suggests that,

> Perhaps non-violence is the difficult practice of letting rage collapse into grief, since then we stand the chance of knowing that *we are bound up with others*, such that who I am or who you are is this living relation that we sometimes lose (Butler 2014, my italics).

It strikes me that the museum is one of the forms we have for slowly *showing what we value* and for *preserving what is left*. And as public social spaces they can demonstrate some ways in which *we are bound up with others*. And perhaps their very boundaries and bindings keep us from driving away quite so fast from the unbearable. After all, the massive museums of capital cities have great long galleries that prevent a quick exit.

I want to do some special pleading for museums, or for their potential, within the context of this special issue about social work and the visual imagination. Not from a place of uncritical affection or professional loyalty, but because they are simply what we have. I will suggest that museums are places for

slowing down

showing what we value

preserving what is left

binding up with others.

§ In the last chapter of *Regarding the Pain of Others* (2003), Susan Sontag considers where photographs of war might best be seen in order to fully contemplate their meaning. She first appears to dismiss museums, for there

> they partake of the fate of all wall-hung or floor-supported art displayed in public spaces. That is, they are stations along a – usually accompanied – stroll. A museum or gallery visit is a social situation, riddled with distractions, in the course of which art is seen and commented on (2003, p. 108).

Furthermore:

> Once a repository for conserving and displaying the fine arts of the past, the museum has become a vast educational institution-cum-emporium, one of whose functions is the exhibition of art (2003, p. 109).

She's right. To retain their public funding museums need to prove that they are not simply indulged anachronisms but socially, educationally and economically useful. Their efforts to do this risk turning them more and more into places of distraction from the art. Maybe, though, the gallery's very 'social situation' makes it apt for the contemplation of suffering. The modern museum tries to preserve things as they have been *and* to be a lively place of changing sociability. This, paradoxically, could be its power: sociability amidst evocations of suffering.

Sontag is no easy friend of museums but she concludes *Regarding the Pain of Others* with a discussion of a 'museum photograph' by the artist Jeff Wall: *Dead Troops Talk (A Vision After an Ambush of a Red Army Patrol near Moqor, Afghanistan, Winter 1986),*[1] (2003). The work is a digital montage in which troops, apparently just killed, appear to engage with each other. She reckons the work demonstrates how 'we' – those who haven't experienced what the troops have gone through – 'can't imagine how dreadful, how terrifying war is; and how normal it becomes' (Sontag 2003, p. 113). Unlike most of the other work described in the book (Goya's *Disasters of War* is the exception) this is not news footage or a press photograph but a photograph made for viewing in a museum. The irony then is that this museum piece demonstrates, albeit with the help of Sontag's interpretation, the unimaginability of war, the limits of the visual imagination. Much of the photographic work that she discusses is made for the press and media, Wall's work is made for museums and like the Goyas only viewable in a museum, if that.

§ Judith Butler's *Frames of War* is an account of how war 'works on the field of the senses' (2009, p. ix). It is about the effects of the presentation of suffering on our responsiveness and how it determines 'what will and will not be a grievable life' (2009, p. 64). Like Sontag she is concerned with how regarding the pain of others in photographs (there is a long section about the digital photographs from Abu Ghraib) might reveal ways to transform the affects of viewing such photographs into effective political action (2009, p. 99). She concludes a chapter on the ethics of photography by briefly picking up Sontag's discussion of *Dead Troops Talk*. She writes that it is Jeff Wall's 'museum piece' that 'allows Sontag to formulate the problem of responding to the pain of others', that is that we can't ever know how dreadful war is. That Sontag uses the 'museum piece' to do this leads Butler to surmise that this

> involves a certain consolidation of the museum world as the one within which she is most likely to find room for reflection and deliberation (2009, 99).

and that it is

> the museum exhibition that gives her the time and space for the kind of thinking and writing she treasures (2009, p. 99).

The question then for advocates of museums is whether they can provide a frame that enables us 'to see what we see', whether they can help us see beyond 'the dehumanising norm, that restricts what is perceivable and, indeed, what can be' (2009, p. 100). Or is the familiar, established norm of the museum too normalising? Butler writes that the circulation of the Abu Graib images outside of the immediate place of their production broke up 'the mechanism of disavowal, scattering grief and outrage in its wake' (2009, p. 100). Can the museum be an ethical messenger as well as an objective reporter and recorder?

Museums decide over and over what will be shown and what will not. Unlike other media, they don't shy away from presenting suffering: remains of the dead figure in many a museum. But the museum's sense of timelessness and its claimed political neutrality can disguise the grievousness and the political sensitivity of what one sees. The media agrees not to print pictures of the war dead but war dead are shown in museums. Museums decide 'what will count within the frame' (Butler 2009, p. 67).

§ Jeff Wall has said that 'art is an independent experience of the world' (Stallabrass 2010, p. 13) and that,

> I don't like the idea of having extra-aesthetic interest in my subjects, as if I am interested in them socially. When I began, I was under the illusion that I did have those interests. I grew up in the 60s and 70s, amid the counter-culture and the New Left, and I still believe a lot of those things, but they don't really apply to my work (Stallabrass 2010, p. 4).

Given Wall's rejection of an 'extra-aesthetic', it's ironic that both Sontag and Butler consider his work within their analyses of war and photography; admittedly this is at the end of chapters, almost an after-thought, but they come with an invitation to take up their line of thinking.

Julian Stallabrass writes that the usefulness for a museum of Wall's photographs is obvious, for they provide 'a form of spectacle that has to be seen as a physical object in a physical space to get the full effect, and as a generator of art-historical discourse' (2010, p. 15). And he agrees that 'they may get us to think about politics or society' (2010, p. 15). But he writes that 'a democratic image culture' can't be found in the museum, 'with its policed and expert discourse' (2010, p17). Whereas YouTube and Flickr offer a 'clearer look into the face of our "actually existing democracy" than the photo-paintings of Wall' (2010, p. 17).

Here's another way to think about museums from John Berger:

> In art museums we come upon the visible of other periods and it offers us company (2001, p. 21).

This 'we', this speaking on behalf of unknown others is annoying, and surprising when it comes from Berger who habitually reveals the details of individual lives. But he's right when he goes on to say that some things – such as teeth, hands, the sun – continue to look the same across millennia, so that when seeing their representations in an art museum

> We feel less alone in face of what we ourselves see each day appearing and disappearing (2001, p. 21).

It isn't just the art works themselves that create links, but that the work is seen in the public space of the museum; inadvertently the museum offers a sociability, a place to gather with others, albeit often in silence, much as therapeutic social work attempts to help people feel less alone.

When regarding the pain of others, one risks bearing the pain forever. The gallery does the bearing for you and will continue to do it forever. Its vast history, space, rationality and materiality are a bulwark against the pain.

§ In a night-time space between the reading of others' accounts of museums and my actual visits I had a dream.

> I am working in the reading room of an archive which is like a large classical gallery in a national museum. A young woman near me, who I remember from the day before,

has two files of documents brought from the store for her to read. I go back to my work and when I next look up she has gone and instead on her table, which is now a plinth as in an exhibition, is a great pile of coins, some unknown old currency. She has left her handbag on the floor by the plinth. Two small children come along and begin to play with the coins and to look in her bag. I take the bag away to keep it safe from them but leave the coins and wonder how long the children will be allowed to play with them before the young woman or a member of staff comes to stop them.

Any idealisation of the museum as a place of free exploration is put paid to in the dream. For here I am, playing amongst all this valuable stuff, whilst I am also on display and acutely aware that the game will end. The contents of the store can be brought out to be unpacked and examined but looking is dangerous and costly. I must take good care and the collections won't release all of their secrets. There are internal and external limits to the visual imagination and to thinking.

§ I went to the exhibition *Conceptual Art in Britain 1964–1979* at Tate Britain.

The first art work you see is by Roelof Louw, *Soul City (Pyramid of Oranges)* (1967). You are invited to take an orange from the pyramid - how novel to be allowed to take something from an exhibition! Rather than openly responding to the invitation I did this furtively. I didn't need an orange, I had food in my bag. Why indulge some artist's fancy that this would be a significant act? But if I leave them they'll only grow mouldy (disaster for a curator) or dry out. Other museums don't allow organic matter into their education rooms let alone in amongst the art works. The caption to the work states 'The full implications of this action are left to the imagination' (Tate Publishing 2016, p. 29). Quite. As though the imagination is some free-flowing thing unaffected by its context.

The final section of the exhibition, called 'Action Practice', shows work by conceptual artists who in the 1970s overtly used their practice to bring about political and social change. Stephen Willats's *Living with Practical Realities* (1978) shows photographs of an elderly woman, Mrs. Moran, who lives alone in a tower block. Willats acted as a kind of artist cum social worker cum sociologist investigating Mrs. Moran's circumstances. The photographs are on three boards along with text and diagrams, in the guise of a sociological essay about the alienated state of such people, or even a social worker's report about Mrs. Moran. There are supposed quotes from Mrs. Moran about her situation:

> For company I usually have to wait until people come to visit me at my place. What do you propose is the way for me to form new relationships within this isolated tower?

The cold language of assessment and the documentary style of the photographs convey something of Mrs. Moran's suffering, this time not the pain of war but of city poverty and isolation. Anne Wagner suggests that Willatts made the work in this way because he knew

> full well that in deploying this cruelly rational apparatus, what is irrational about Mrs. Moran's unbearable isolation will be laid bare (2016, p. 21).

Transposed to the gallery from an imaginary sociology book or a social worker's report, perhaps it hits one all the harder. The contrasts between the gallery's rich grandeur and the life of Mrs. Moran are disturbing, maybe not enough to provoke action, but they provoke sympathy. She's noticed. Or maybe in fact the *impossibility* of knowing her unbearable isolation is laid bear.

§ Earlier in the day I had shown my passport (photo evidence of who I am was required) in order to enter the Prints and Drawings Room where I'd arranged to see another Jeff Wall photograph, *A Sapling Held by a Post* (2000). He was commissioned, along with nine other photographic artists, to make a work to celebrate the opening of Tate Modern in May 2000.

Viewing the work in the Prints and Drawings Room is moons away from Sontag's distracted walk through the gallery. It's laid out for you in advance on a fine wooden stand in a stately room set aside for viewing work; there are murmurings from a few other viewers and staff, but essentially you and the work are in private within this public place. There's a basin for washing your hands. You are there to study the formal work. In this setting it is above all a work of art, its affective powers or any social accounting it might do is diminished by the aura of art history. Oh the reverence of looking in this place!

My eye is drawn not to the sapling or the post but to the strip of heavy fabric, twisted in the middle, the colour of bandage, which wraps the sapling and the post together. A thread hangs from an unravelled edge of the fabric and winds around the sapling like a tendril of a climbing plant, but with not so tight a twist as honeysuckle. A nail through the fabric into the post is rusting. For now the bandage holds the sapling which will soon be free of its support and allowed to grow alone. The post will bear the imprint of support through the stain of rust and the hole made by the nail. Knots on the vulnerable sapling are like straightened-out elbows.

§ Another day I visited Tate Stores in Southwark. This is where the works in the Tate Collection are stored away when they are not displayed, and is not to be confused with Tate Store, the shop. Visitors with an appointment are welcomed at Tate Stores. Here the work of keeping and preserving art – the cataloguing, storing, cleaning, conserving and so on - isn't hidden away as it is in public galleries, here it is evident. The work is evident but the works of art are hidden behind wrappings or in crates.

I have come to see another Jeff Hill work, *Study for 'A Sudden Gust of Wind (After Hokusai)'* (1993) which is itself a testimony to the work of making art. It is a collage of photocopied paper and photographs that he assembled in the process of making the final piece. This time I crouched down on the floor of the store to look at the work, still with bubble wrap around its frame.

The composition follows that of a woodcut, *Travellers Caught in a Sudden Breeze at Ejiri* (c.1832) by Katsushika Hokusai (1760–1849). Both pictures are of a landscape in which a woman's sheaf of papers is blown away from her hands by the wind, some rise high up into the sky. It depicts just what the museum store works to prevent – loss of precious work by accident or climate. It reveals the painstaking work Hill did in order to make the final work. The store also reveals some of the painstaking tasks of preserving a work once it's made and judged worthy of being kept in perpetuity.

The workings of artists, of art handlers, conservators, curators, cleaners, security staff can't normally be seen. It's as though in order to best view the art work itself all trace of how it's made and how it's preserved inside the institution has to be removed. Some kind of purity of form, purity of existence, is sought in order to better view an essence.

In the store, in any museum store, the works are wrapped up within their own melancholy. You can see them lined up along the shelves, but not see them. The store is the heartland of the museum, a functional, out-of-the-way place of work but also a place of silence where little appears to happen. It's waiting for some future when its work will be realised, comprehended.

Or maybe the keeping of it all here, the knowing at some level that it's here, is enough to give the nation and its citizens some sense of value, pride, hope for the future. It's all in the bank: an investment in knowledge, beauty and authenticity. This work is worth preserving.

§ The next day in Tate Modern I saw an exhibition of the work of Mona Hatoum. In this exhibition you are away from the distractions of the modern gallery, you can find a distance from the suffering, and as a result somehow see it all the more. In one work, *Quarters* (1996), institutional metal bunk beds are stripped of any comforting mattress and blanket. They wait for a response. As with anything, you can walk on by, or stop. If you stop you might find an account of the world in a visual and material language that takes you by surprise, you might also find some kind of account of yourself. The work provoked thoughts in me about the preservation of objects and of life, of being prone, lying down for rest or for a restless night. A bed without comfort signals torture; abstractions become metal in the materiality.

Of another of her works in the exhibition, *Undercurrent (red)* (2008), Hatoum has written that it creates a 'breathing pace', thereby suggesting both a space and a slowing down to a rhythmical heart and lung pace. Not an empty space (no such thing exists), but movement, a receptivity to one's own body and maybe then to the bodies of others. I tried to breath in time to the work's breath, to stay in the discomforting place, not drive myself away. When I did leave I took with me a greater sense of fragility, danger and of how weaponry might be used against me or others. In a museum those of us who don't live in a war zone might get some tiny sense of what it could be like to do so. But as I left I remembered Sontag's contempt for the Imperial War Museum's 'Trench Experience' and 'Blitz Experience' (2003, p. 109) that also attempt to do this. It could be that it's the latter's overt designs on the visitor that are the problem. The museum's presumption.

§ Back in Tate Britain, it's almost six o'clock and staff heave internal doors closed and guide the remaining visitors towards the exit. If we want more we'll have to come back again to find works that might still be there or might have gone back into the store or on tour around the world. The night-time security will be mounted and the gallery will settle back into a silent space. The space and pace are here every day and can be used, or not. It is no neutral space, it's riven with the museum's purpose. It is as opaque as the human subject, a dense mass of stone, paper, metal, plastic, wood. Pockets can be found where one might sense oneself and the world differently.

Mona Hatoum has said

I want the work in the first instance to have a strong formal presence, and through the physical experience to activate a psychological and emotional response (Tate 2016).

The museum itself, certainly one like Tate, has a massively strong formal presence that can comfort, awaken, intimidate; you can't escape its institutional might. This might persist despite the lack of consensus on what a museum is for. There is a collective ethos about the value of a museum's work of preserving objects since this speaks to primitive, shared desires for continuity. But the idealisation of the museum as a holder of knowledge no longer holds sway and other roles are sought for it, one of these is as a container of the actual and the imaginary.

§ Read this extract from Berger's *A Fortunate Man* (1967) and in your imagination try replacing the word 'doctor' with 'museum':

> The doctor is the familiar of death. When we call for a doctor, we are asking him to cure us and to relieve our suffering, but, if he cannot cure us, we are also asking him to witness our dying. The value of the witness is that he has seen so many others die ... He is the living intermediary between us and the multitudinous dead (p. 62).

The 'multitudinous dead' are housed in the museum, either in the form of 'human remains' or, more imaginatively, in all those millions of objects removed from everyday life to be kept forever in museums. Berger goes on to say that it would be a mistake to conclude from this that the patient wants a *friendly* doctor: 'His hopes and demands ... however undeclared even to himself, are much more profound and precise (p. 62). Profundity and precision can be found in a museum. The best offer friendliness as well, but never at the expense of a witnessing of something more profound.

Note

1. The irony is that this 'museum piece' was sold from a private collection in 2012 for $3.6M US. http://www.cbc.ca/news/arts/jeff-wall-photograph-sells-for-record-3-6m-us-1.1205822.

References

Berger, J. (1967). *A fortunate man*. London: Penguin.
Berger, J. (2001). *The shape of a pocket*. London: Bloomsbury.
Butler, J. (2005). *Giving an account of oneself*. New York, NY: Fordham University Press.
Butler, J. (2009). *Frames of war: When is life grievable?* Brooklyn, NY: Verso.
Butler, J. (2014). *Speaking of rage and grief*. Retrieved May 30, 2016, from https://www.youtube.com/watch?v=ZxyabzopQi8
Sontag, S. (2003). *Regarding the pain of others*. London: Penguin.
Stallabrass, J. (2010). Museum photography and museum prose. *New Left Review, 65*, 93–125.
Tate (Exhibition Guide). (2016). *Mona Hatoum 4 May – 21 August 2016*. London: Tate.
Tate Publishing. (2016). *Conceptual art in Britain. 1964–1979*. London: Author.
Wagner, A. (2016, July 14). At Tate Britain. *London Review of Books*, 20–21.

AFTERWORD

We hope you have enjoyed the virtual collection of visual images we have gathered together in this special edition and that some will remain in your mind's eye and your imagination. Reaching 'the end' of some galleries and exhibitions one is sometimes drawn to return to pieces viewed previously, to take another look, and maybe to think about why that or those pieces in particular made the impression that they did. Sometimes one returns with the intention of 'fixing' an image more firmly in the mind so that it lasts for longer or could be recalled when wanted. We hope readers will go back to some of these articles or parts of them in a similar way and see whether new things emerge as if seen for the first time. One of the themes throughout this collection of articles has been the collaborative and shared nature of seeing and we would be pleased if you would like to let us know your views on anything you have read here in order to develop and enhance the shared experience. Please contact the editors if you would like to do this.

References

Alma, D. (Ed.). (2015). *The emergency poet: An anti-stress poetry anthology*. London: Michael O'Mara Books.

Benjamin, J. (1988). *The bonds of love*. New York, NY: Pantheon.

Chamberlayne, P., & Smith, M. (2009). *Art, creativity and imagination in social work practice*. Abingdon: Routledge.

England, H. (1986). *Social work as art*. London: Allen and Unwin.

Goodwin, D. (Ed.). (2000). *101 Poems to get you through the day and night: A survival kit for modern life*. London: Harper Collins.

Gosso, S. (2004). *Psychoanalysis and art*. London: Karnac.

Glover, N. (2009). *Psychoanalytic aesthetics*. London: Karnac.

Gunaratnam, Y. (2015). *Death and the migrant: Bodies, borders and care*. London: Bloomsbury.

Langer, S. K. (1948/1942). *Philosophy in a new key: A study in the symbolism of reason, rite, and art*. New York, NY: NAL Mentor.

O'Neill, M (1999). *Adorno, culture and feminism*. London: Sage.

O'Neill, M. (2001). *Prostitution and feminism: Towards a politics of feeling*. Cambridge: Polity Press.

Roy, A. (2017). Mobility and the scenic intelligibility of social work. *Qualitative Social Work, 16*, 2–13.

Roy, A., Hughes, J., Froggett, L., & Christensen, J. (2015). Using mobile methods to explore the lives of marginalised young men in Manchester. In L. Hardwick, R. Smith, & A. Worsley (Eds.), *Innovations in social work research* (pp. 153–170). London: Jessica Kingsley Publishers.

Index

Note: Page numbers in *italics* refer to figures
Page numbers in **bold** refer to tables
Page numbers followed by 'n' refer to notes

action inquiry: reasons for 22–3; working with poetic 23–5
addiction, and recovery 79
aesthetic intelligence 1
'aesthetic third' 114, 115, 116
affect 116, 140
ageing, challenges of 39–42
allegory: and images 77–8; and movement 80–6
The Allegory of Love (Lewis) 85
Alma, Deborah 19
Alzheimer's disease 41
Andersson, J. 41–2
anxieties: containing 62–3; defences against 62–3; of older adults 40–4, 49–50
apprenticeships 141–2
'The Archers' 116, 119n3
Aristotle 116
art(s): and crafts 135–7, 141, 143; as independent experience of the world 152; objects 114; as play 143; practices 117; producing affects and intensities 140; as sensation based experience 139; and social work 135–44; training in 112–13
art curating, with sexually exploited young people 111–19
artefacts, and its relationship to imagination 114–17
artists 81
art objects, transformative power of 109
art projects, socially engaged 130
arts-based methods 24, 96
Attachment Theory 14
auto-ethnographic methods 124

balance, use of term 31
BASE (Barnardo's Against Sexual Exploitation) project 112, 119n2
Bauman, Z. 103–4
Behuniak, S. M. 51
Bell, K. 137
Benjamin, J. 143

Benjamin, Walter 77–8, 96
Berger, John 1, 152, 156
Bergson, H. 63
bilddenken (thinking in images) 96
biographies *see* walking biographies
Bion, W. R. 43, 51n5
bodies: and image space 96–7; experience, in movement 76
Bowlby, John 14
Braidotti, R. 76–7
Bredin, K. 57
Brough, P. 26, 27, 32
Butler, Judith 149, 151

The Canadian Partnerships in Dementia Care Alliance 41
The Canal & Rivers Trust 124
care, and social work 139, 143
Carlisle, P. 14
'catastrophic thinking' 11
Chamberlain, K. 95
Chamberlayne, Prue 1
change management 27
Cheston, C. 57
Cheston, R. 65
child sexual exploitation (CSE) 109, 112–13
Christensen, J. 91
Christopher, G. 57
Clarke, Carrie 55, 57, *60*
cognitive behavioural therapy 11
The Cold Truth exhibition 111–19
collective poems 24, 28–9
Collins, K. M. 31
Conceptual Art in Britain exhibition 153
Conversation Pieces (Kester) 123
'corps exquis' form 24, 31
Creative People and Places (CCP) 124
creative relations 123–32
Crociani-Windland, Lita 69, 133, 135
'cruel optimism' 76

Cullen, A. 95
Cunliffe, A. L. 33–4
curator 119n1

dance 76–7
The Danish Dementia Alliance 41
Dead Troops Talk (Wall) 151
death: life and 41–2, 47–9; instinct 9
Deleuze, G. 76–7, 86, 135–44
dementia 5, 40–1, 46–7; containing anxiety 62–3;
    dream 61–2; ethics approval and consent 58;
    findings, emergent themes 63–7; fluidity 69–70;
    harvest-time, as embodiment of relationship
    66–7; language, as conscious/unconscious
    communication 67–9; life-story film 60; loss
    63–4; memory and time, nature of 63;
    methodology 58–9; non-linearity 62; person-
    centred care 57, 59; re-imagining, using visual
    matrix 55, 57–71; refugees and evacuation 65–6;
    relationships 64–5; sample selection 58; setting
    the scene 59–60; specific value of visual matrix 70
depersonalisation 63
depressive mode, of experience 44
depressive position 12
dialogical aesthetics 123, 129
difference and repetition 136–8, 142
discursive space 131
disguised compliance 9
dissonances, resonances and 59, 67
distress, social workers' experience of 11, 13
dreams 61–2
Duff, C. 140

elasticity, sense of 69
The Emergency Poet: An Anti-Stress Poetry Anthology
    (Alma) 19
emotions, conflicting 63
empathetic responses 114
end-of-life care 41
England, H. 1
epistemology 135
Eros 9
ethno-mimesis: defined 89, 92; as performative
    praxis 92–3
evacuation, refugees and 65–6
expertise 141
*Exploring Life Transitions in Old Age through a Visual
    Matrix* 39

Fallen Angels Dance Theatre (FADT), and people in
    recovery from substance misuse 75–80
fear 41; in social work 13
feeling, thought and 43, 44, 59, 92
Ferguson, H. 103
fluidity 69–70
A Fortunate Man (Berger) 156
Frames of War (Butler) 151
French, R. 65, 70

Freud, S. 115
Froggett, Lynn 1, 39, 58, 59, 62, 91, 114, 157

Giving an Account of Oneself (Butler) 149
Goffman, I. 136
Goodwin, Daisy 19
Greenhaus, J. H. 31
Gripsrud, Birgitta H. 39
Grisoni, Louise 19, 21
Groot, S. 95
Grosz, E. 142
Guattari, F. 140, 141, 144

Hall, T. 95
Hansebo, G. 41–2
Hartley, C. 14
Hatoum, Mona 155
Haughton, H. 115
health 140, 143
healthcare environments, unconscious processes in 63
helplines, telephone 116, 119n4
Hodgetts, D. 95
Hoeppner, B. 79
Hokusai, Katsushika 154
Hollway, Wendy 39, 62
home carers, male 124–32
homelessness, visualising 95, 96
Hubbard, P. 95
Hughes, J. 91
hylomorphism 123, 131

identity 136–8
Immanence: A Life (Deleuze) 138
immersion: benefits of community 79; in lived
    cultures 92, 97
indwelling 128–9
Ingold, Tim 76–7, 79–80, 86, 105n1, 123, 129, 131
insight 1
'intuition in action' 130
Ismail, S. 57

Johnson, M. 31, 33
The Journal of Social Work Practice 1
Jung, Carl 79, 115

Kahlo, Frida 149
Kaliath, T. 26, 27, 32
Kelly, J. F. 79
Kester, Grant 123–4, 129, 131
Kitwood, T. 57
Klein, M. 8, 9, 12; psychoanalytic theory 44, 49
knowledge, and recovery 79–80
Kundera, Milan 104

Lading, Ase 39
Lady Macbeth (character) 6–13
Lakoff, G. 31, 33
Langer, Suzanne 2, 51n4

language, as conscious/unconscious communication 67–9
Lawrence, Gordon 61
Lee, C. 14
Lewis, C.S. 85
life: and death 41–2, 47–9; Deleuzian concept of 138–9
'life-story film' perceptions of people with dementia 57–71
liminal space 70, 114
Little, R. 114
Liveng, Anne 39
Living with Practical Realities (Willats) 153
Lloyd, L. 41
Louw, Roelof 153

Macbeth (Shakespeare), relevance to social work practice 5–16
Making: Anthropology, Archeology, Art and Architecture (Ingold) 123
male home carers 124–32
Malone, Eloise 109, 111
Manley, Julian 1, 39, 58, 59, 61, 70, 75, 157
Matarasso, Francois 118
maternal instinct 8
McCall-Smith, Alexander 141
McHugh, Catrina 91, 92–3
Mclintock, D. 115
memory, and time 63
Men Who Care project 124, 129
mental health social workers, views and experiences of 14
Menzies-Lyth, E. 62–3
Mestrovic, S. G. 96
metaphors: structural 31; in dreams 61
mobile methods 91, 103
morphogenesis 123, 131
movement: and allegory 80–6; concept of 77; and dance 80
Multi Agency Child Sexual Exploitation group 116
museums, relevance for social work 149–56

nomadic theory 76

Obholzer, A. 63
old age: transitions and visual matrix method 39–51
101 Poems to get you through the day and night (Goodwin) 19
O'Neill, Maggie 91
ontology 135
Open Clasp Theatre 92, 105n1
organisational changes 28
The Origin of Tragic German Drama (Benjamin) 78
Österlind, J. 41–2
outreach workers 95

Pagano, M. 79
paranoid schizoid position 12, 44, 67

Peak, J. 65
person-centred dementia care 57, 59
photographs 95, 150, 151–2, 153–4
Pleschberger, S. 41
poems, collective 24, 28–9
poetic action inquiry 23–5
poetry 21–2; challenges of work–life balance through 27–31; workshops 27; visual imagination in 31–4
policies 40
post emotional society, concept of 96
'pre-individual singularity' 139
'pre-subjective delirium' 139
provocations 59, 67

qualification 140
Quarters (Hatoum) 155
quasi-therapeutic effect 55, 62

Radiant Gallery 111
Radley, A. 95
Ramvi, Ellen 39
re-remembering 63
recovery from substance misuse 75; allegory 77–8, 80–6; dance 76; interrelationality 77; journeys, directions and destinations 75; methodology 80; and movement 76–86; trauma/knowing 79–80; in treatment sector 78–9; using visual matrix 76; wayfaring 76; working with FADT 75–80
reflexivity, understanding of 22
refugees, and evacuation 65–6
Regarding the pain of others (Sontag) 150–1
religion, and spirituality 14
repetition, difference and 136–8, 142
research 12–15
resonances, and dissonances 59, 67
retirement 40, 45–6
'rhizome': Deleuzian concept of 76; scenic, concept of 62
risk assessments 7–8
Roberts, V. 63
Robertson, James 13–14
Robertson, Joyce 13
Roy, Alastair 1, 58, 59, 61, 70, 75, 91, 114, 157
'rule of optimism' 9

sameness 137
A Sapling Held by a Post 154
Sauvagnargues, A. 141
seeing, in social work traditions 13
self, reflection of 127
senile dementia 5
sensation 85, 139
'sensuous knowing' 97
sexual exploitation 112
Shaw, J. D. 31
'Shed Life Ways' 124
shed space 124

silence, discourse of 41–2
Simpson, P. 65, 70
Smith, Martin 1, 3, 5, 157
Smith, R. 95
sociability 152
social dreaming 61
social justice 96–7
social research 92
social unconscious, concept of 62
social work: art and 135–44; care and 139, 143; fear
    in 13; *Macbeth* (Shakespeare), relevance to 5–16;
    museums relevance for 149–56; traditions, seeing
    in 13; as work on the move 103
Social work as art (England) 1
social workers: experience of distress 11, 13; mental
    health, views and experiences of 14
social work practice 3; disguised compliance 9;
    elements of 7–10; risk assessments 7–8; 'thinking
    the unthinkable' 8
'societal-collective processes' 62
Sontag, Susan 150–1
Soul City (Pyramid of Oranges) (Louw) 153
'Speaking of Rage and Grief' (Butler) 149
'spiritual midwifery' 70
spirituality 14, 81–2
splitting 43–4, 62, 67, **68**
'spoiled identity' 136
Stallabrass, Julian 152
Stolte, O. 95
Stout, R. L. 79
structural metaphors 31
Study for 'A Sudden Gust of Wind (After Hokusai)' (Hill)
    154
substance misuse *see* recovery from substance misuse
Substance Use Recovery Evaluator tool 78
supervision 10–12
Sutton, E. 41
sympathetic responses 114

Taussig, M. 97
Ternestedt, B.-M. 41–2
theatres 92, 93, 95, 96–7, 103, 104, 105n2; and
    walk shops 93–6, 102–3
Thorne, K. 65
thought, and feeling 43, 44, 59, 92
time, memory and 63
Titley, William 121, 123
Torbert, W. 22
training, young people as artists and curators112–13
Transgressive Imaginations: crime, deviance and culture 103
transitions: from life to death 41–2, 47–9; from
    mental functioning to dementia 40–1, 46–7; from
    working life to retirement 40, 45–6

trauma, and recovery 79–80
Travellers Caught in a Sudden Breeze at Ejiri (Hokusai)
    154
Tree of Knowledge 45, 46
Trustram, Myna 114, 147, 149
The Two and a Half Pillars of Wisdom (McCall-Smith)
    141

UK Drug Policy Commission 78
uncanny, Freud's concept of 109, 115
the unconscious 3, 13, 141
Undercurrent (red) (Hatoum) 155

virtuality 140
visual imagination: as art and craft activities 135;
    examining in work-life balance poetry 31–4; in
    Macbeth 5–16; and reflexivity, in poetry creation
    21–34
visual matrix methodology 2, 37; ageing/splitting
    and 43–4; allegory/movement in 80–4;
    challenges of ageing 39–42; finding patterns in
    data 44–9; implications for 42–3; re-imagining
    dementia using 55, 57–71; specific value of 70;
    transitions in old age through 39–51; using for
    recovery 76; using to generating data 42–3

Wagner, Anne 153
walking biographies 92–3, *97–105*
walk shops, theatres and 93–6, 102–3
Wall, Jeff 151–2, 154
'War Horse' (film) 65
wayfaring 76
Whitaker, L. 114
Whitby, P. 65
White, K. 41
Whyte, D. 22
Willats, Stephen 153
Winnicott, D. 65, 114
women: body and image space 96–7; complexity of
    life of 91–104; maps providing sense of
    experiences 94–6; theatre and walk shop 93–6;
    walking biographies 92–3, *97–105*
work-life balance: action inquiry, reasons for 22;
    challenges of 25–7; within change management
    context 21–34; defined 27; illustrating challenges
    through poetry 27–31; poetic action inquiry,
    working with 23–5; poetry, visual imagination in
    31–4; six conceptualisations of 26–7

Yggdrasill tree 46, 51n8
young people: recovery from sexual exploitation 112

Zeisel, J. 57